WORDS AND NAMES

WORDS AND NAMES

BY ERNEST WEEKLEY, M.A.

'Emblem reduceth conceits intellectual
to images sensible.'—Bacon.

LONDON
JOHN MURRAY, ALBEMARLE STREET, W.

'Percontatorem fugito: nam garrulus idem est.'
HORACE.

FIRST EDITION . . . *October* 1932
Reprinted . . . . . *January* 1933

CONTENTS

PREFACE

THIS book, now offered as the promised sequel to my Words Ancient and Modern and More Words Ancient and Modern, badly needs an apology, for I am acutely conscious of its scrappy and unsystematic nature. In the Preface to my Etymological Dictionary of Modern English I ventured to express the opinion that the part played by personal names in the creation of our vocabulary is not yet realized by etymologists, and it has long been my intention to write something about the English language on the scale of Migliorini's admirable work Dal Nome Proprio al Nome Comune. The material accumulated during many years has proved unmanageable in bulk, and time is not available for reducing it to order. Moreover, there is in English a complete lack of those *Vorarbeiten* which are of so much help to Continental scholars. So, despairing of carrying out my original intention, I have made a rather haphazard selection from a chaos of miscellaneous facts and allowed my pen to run on without any close regard to the rather vague headings of the various chapters. The result is very uneven, e.g. there is a striking disparity between the rather out-of-the-way information which is contained in some of the chapters and the commonplace Biblical and mythological allusions scattered throughout the book. My excuse for including a sprinkling of the latter is that the post-War generation knows little of Holy Writ and nothing of the Ancient World, so that the commonplace allusions of the 19th century are on the way to become recondite mysteries. Perhaps the book, with all its manifest imperfections, may amuse some of those who have been good enough to like my earlier works, and I cherish the hope that it may induce some of our younger scholars to devote themselves to a more erudite examination of special aspects of the subject.

ERNEST WEEKLEY.

UNIVERSITY COLLEGE,
    NOTTINGHAM.
        July, 1932.

CHAPTER I

WORDS AND NAMES

A GREAT deal has been written by Continental philologists on the difference, or lack of difference, between nouns proper and nouns common, and on the influences which cause a word to pass from one class into the other.[1] In English it is usual to take the initial capital as the criterion. *Guy*, as the baptismal name of the redoubtable Fawkes, is a proper noun, but the same word, becoming, after a long succession of bonfire night celebrations, synonymous with a grotesque figure, loses the big *G* and becomes a common noun, eventually acquiring in the United States the sense of chap, fellow. The verb to *guy*, originally to deride an unsatisfactory actor, is also American. Similarly the Spanish name *Diego*, equivalent to *Jago* or *James*, is written with a small *d* when, in the form *dago*, it is used as a nickname for a southern European of Latin race, and the abbreviated *Reuben*,

---

[1] The literature on the subject is immense. Two books from which I have borrowed examples are Migliorini, Dal Nome Proprio al Nome Comune (Geneva, 1927), a comprehensive survey of this element in the Romance languages, and Peterson, Le Passage Populaire des Noms de Personne à l'État de Noms Communs (Uppsala, 1929), which deals especially with the figurative use of baptismal names in French.

taken as a typical name for an American rustic, a
hick, is usually spelt *rube*.   *Hick* itself is one of the
large class of words which, long obsolete in England,
still flourish in the United States.   It is a pet-form
of *Richard*,[1] used, like *Hodge* [2] or *Giles*,[2] for a simple-
minded chawbacon.   The Oxford Dictionary quotes
from one of Steele's forgotten comedies (1702),
' Richard Bumpkin !   Ha !   A perfect country Hick '.

As this book will consist chiefly of digressions,
we will begin with a digression on the name *Guy*,
borne by many famous medieval warriors, but
unpopular in England since 1605.   It comes, via
Old French, from a Latin *Vitus*, a rather hazy saint,
said to have been martyred under Diocletian.   His
connection with the dance, French *danse de Saint-
Guy*, German *Veitstanz*, is not explained, though a
plausible theory connects it with the heathen
evolutions round the Midsummer Eve bonfire.   In
its German form the name was familiarly applied
to the Swiss mercenary of the 16th century, *Bruder
Veit*.   Italian *guidone* means a rogue.   The medieval
Latin form was *Wido* and a diminutive survives in
the surname *Wyatt*.

The idea that governs our rather illogical use of
the capital letter seems to be that a proper name
is a meaningless label and only becomes a real word
when it is used in a transferred sense and applied
to a type, class or some sort of object connected

---

[1] Richard II. is called *Hick Heavyhead* in Richard the Redeless.

[2] *Hodge* is a pet form of *Roger*, and has been used of a rustic
since the 16th century.   *Giles* comes, via French *Gilles*, stock
name for a stage simpleton, from Greco-Latin *Aegidius* (which
looks curious, but is quite true).

with the name. At *Bridewell*, i.e. St. Bridget's Well, London, was a royal dwelling which Edward VI. converted into a hospital. Later it became a house of correction, and the name was imitated in many provincial towns which still have their *bridewells*, or gaols. As early as the 16th century English invalids were accustomed to take a cure at *Spa*, in Belgium, usually referred to as ' the Spa ', i.e. the spring, just as Bath was called ' the Bath '—

> Th' English Bath and eke the German Spau.
> (Faerie Queene, I. xi. 30.)

Since the later 18th century the name has been given to watering-places in general and has long since become the common noun *spa*. An early parallel is *labyrinth*, the proper name of the Cretan maze constructed by Daedalus and from which Theseus escaped by the help of Ariadne's ' clew [1] of thread '. Another is *meander*, now usually a verb, from *Maeander*, a winding river of Phrygia. An imitation of this is *Scamander* (the name of a river of the Troad), similarly used in 19th-century slang, and surviving in the Yorkshire *skimaunder*. There was originally only one *archipelago*, lit. chief sea, studded with the isles of Greece, and one Jewish *ghetto*, that of Venice.

The obsolete *hansom* began its career in 1834 as ' Hansom's patent '. The ' Macintosh capes and cloaks ' made from a waterproof fabric patented by *Charles Macintosh* in 1823 are now simply (with an incorrect spelling) *mackintoshes*. Per contra, *Burberry* is not a common noun, and must not be spelt

[1] Whence the Sherlockian *clue*.

with a small ' b '. We usually write *french-polisher*, *french-window*, and the nautical *flemish-coil*, now that the adjectives no longer carry their national significance, while *turkey* and *guinea-pig* have long ceased to call up the names of the countries with which they were once erroneously associated.[1] In French an *Amazone* is a member of a tribe of war-like females described by Herodotus, the name meaning (perhaps by folk-etymology) breastless, because the *Amazons* were fabled to cut off the right breast for convenience in archery ; an *amazone* is a lady rider, and, by extension, a lady's riding-habit. *Céladon* was a languishing shepherd in d'Urfé's pastoral romance Astrée (1610), but, when used by collectors of china to describe the pale green he affected, the name is spelt in French and English without a capital. But the capital letter is really no criterion.[2] We may say that Hercules and Mr. Henry Ford are proper names, but when we say that a man is a regular *Hercules* or talk of buying a second-hand *Ford*, we are really using common nouns. And here it may be remarked that, with the infinite multiplication of new types of aeroplanes, motor-cars, fire-arms, cocktails, and other death-dealing devices, the initial capital tends more and more to resist elimination.

The fact is that there is no dividing line between the two classes of words. A common phenomenon in European speech, and one which has occupied

---

[1] On these two words see my Romance of Words (pp. 51–2).

[2] Nor is it possible, in this region of language, to observe consistency in the matter of the initial capital. Hence the irregularities to be noticed in this book.

many eminent philologists, is the conversion of the proper name into a common noun ; but, if we go back to the earliest proper names of which we have record, we find the process reversed. All names were originally significant. The heathen gods and goddesses, so far as etymology can track them, are personifications of the forces of nature or of the chief passions that sway mankind. Thus *deity*, *divine*, *Diana*, *Jupiter* (*Dyeu pater*), and *Zeus* are all cognate with Latin *dies*, day, and with an Aryan root that means bright, shining. *Eros* and *Cupid* are Greek and Latin names for sexual desire. *Venus* means love, attraction, and is ultimately cognate with *wish*. From it is formed the verb *venerari*, to adore, cherish, so that the adjectives *venerable* and *venereal* go back to a common source. *Psyche* is Greek for soul. *Psyche task*, one impossible of accomplishment, is from the punishment inflicted by Venus on Psyche for daring to love Cupid. *Nemesis*, the Greek goddess of retribution, is an abstract noun from *nemein*, to apportion a due. *Themis*, a personification of justice, is the thing ' set ' ; cf. Anglo-Saxon *gesetnes*, law, and German *gesetz*. *Pomona*, goddess of fruit, is the apple-woman, her name being formed from *pomum*, as that of *Bellona*, goddess of war, from *bellum*. *Vesta*, whose eternal flame was guarded by the *vestal* virgins, is the Latin form of Greek *hestia*, hearth. With a small *v* she became, in the 19th century, a wax match, *Lucifer*, the morning-star, having already been appropriated by the wooden variety. *Iris* is the Greek for rainbow, and *Echo*, a personifi-

cation of the Greek word for sound, is less imaginative than the Old Norse *dvergmal*, dwarf-talk, from
the mountain gnomes who were supposed to answer
shouts. The Greek *hēbē*, freshness of youth, became
the name of the cup-bearer of the gods and eventually English for a barmaid.

The same is true of the various non-divine figures
of ancient mythology. The name of the original
Sibyl, Greek *Sibulla*, is (says Jerome) a Doric form
of the Attic *theoboulē*, i.e. divine will. *Daedalus*,
Greek *daidalos*, the cunning worker, is the personification of craftsmanship. His most famous effort
(p. 3) is perpetuated in French *dédale*, a maze.
Tantalus, who, for an offence which is variously
described, was condemned to eternal thirst in the
presence of water and refreshing fruit, survives in
tantalize, in the *tantalus* spirit-stand, inaccessible
without the key, and the chemical *tantalum*, which
cannot absorb acid when immersed in it. His name
belongs to an Aryan root meaning to endure.
Prometheus, lit. the foreseeing or prudent, was the
Titan who, for bestowing on man the gift of fire,
was chained by Zeus on Mount Caucasus, where
an eagle daily devoured his liver. He is the personification of man's protest against the tyranny
of the gods. The *Sphinx*, which propounded riddles
to the Thebans and strangled the unsuccessful, is
Greek for throttler, and *Oedipus*, who guessed right,
means ' swollen foot ', equivalent to the English
name *Puddifoot*. Attica had a legendary bandit
named *Procrustes*, who, by stretching or chopping,
made his captives fit his bed ; hence *Procrustean*,

'aiming to produce uniformity by violent or arbitrary methods' (Oxford Dictionary) ; but *Procrustes* simply means stretcher. In the Odyssey Minerva assumed the form and name of *Mentor*, which probably meant adviser, 'monitor'. Chiefly through the important part played by *Mentor* in Fénelon's Télémaque, the name has gradually shed the capital and become again what it no doubt was originally, i.e. a common noun. The *Myrmidons* were a Thessalian tribe who accompanied Achilles to the siege of Troy. A *myrmidon* is, with a gradual decline, a faithful attendant, an unscrupulous henchman or hired ruffian, a police-officer of the baser sort, 'myrmidon of the law'. But the original *Myrmidons* were ant-men (Greek *murmēx*, ant) and belong to some nature-myth far older than the Iliad. *Hector* in Greek means upholder ; he was the 'prop of Troy'. He has now become a verb (p. 78).

Our personal names and place-names have gone through similar vicissitudes. *George* goes back to Greek *geōrgos*, a farmer, lit. earthworker, whose activities are described in Virgil's *Georgics*. *Charles* is a Teutonic name, ultimately identical with *churl* and with modern German *kerl*, chap, fellow. Via the fame of Charlemagne it has given the Russian *korol*, king, while the *carl's wain*, the constellation of the Great Bear, which came to us from Old Norse, has been converted, under the same historic influence, into *Charles's wain*.[1]

When we speak of a ripe *stilton*, we do not think

---

[1] This was partly due to our ancestors' confusing *Arcturus*, from Greek *arctos*, bear, with *Arthur*, and *Arthur* with *Charlemagne*.

of a place, but of a cheese. A few years ago a London magistrate, dealing with some disputed trade description, observed sagely, ' Not all Stilton cheese is made at Stilton.' He might have gone further and have said that no Stilton cheese has ever been made at Stilton. This delicacy comes from the Vale of Belvoir, Leicestershire. In the 18th century a famous coaching-inn at Stilton, Huntingdonshire, was kept by a man from the Belvoir country, who regularly imported his native cheese for the delectation of his customers. Hence it became known as *Stilton cheese*. *Stilton* itself, before it became a proper name, was the *stigol* [1]*-tun*, or fenced homestead, of some Anglo-Saxon peasant.

Transporting ourselves once more to Greece, we find that there was originally only one *academy*, the grove at Athens (named from some prehistoric *Academus*) where Plato taught his disciples, and one *lyceum*,[2] the garden, near the temple of Apollo, where Aristotle lectured. The original *athenaeum* was the temple of *Athene*, where professors and orators held forth. There were plenty of porches and colonnades at Athens, but one of them, the *stoa poikilē*, or Painted Porch, where Zeno taught, became ' The Porch ' and is immortalized in the word *stoic*—

> See there the olive grove of Academe,
> Plato's retirement, where the Attic bird
> Trills her thick-warbl'd notes the summer long . . .
>   within the walls then view
> The Schools of antient sages ; his who bred
> Great Alexander to subdue the world,
> Lyceum there and painted Stoa next.
>   (Par. Reg., iv. 244.)

---

[1] Hence modern *stile*.   [2] From *Lyceus*, an epithet of Apollo.

There was even, for the ancient world, only one *volcano*, viz. Etna, in the bowels of which *Vulcan* and the Cyclopes forged the thunderbolts of Jupiter.

One could go on indefinitely with examples showing the very shadowy nature of the boundary that divides the proper name from the common noun, but it is time to come to the real subject under discussion, viz. the way in which, within the experience of our own language, names have contributed to our everyday vocabulary. This may happen in various ways. Probably the greatest number of such words are names of objects or products associated with special geographical names. Words of this type are almost innumerable, of no great philological interest and usually easy to trace. Some places seem to have been especially favoured, e.g. *Bath*, with its *bun, chair, stone, brick, chap* and *Oliver*, the last being a biscuit named from a well-known Bath doctor, just as the less palatable *abernethy* bears the name of a physician (*John Abernethy*, + 1831) equally famous for his dietary theories and his brusqueness. An example from the East is *Damascus*, to which we owe *damask*, the *damask rose, damascened* steel and the *damson*. Such appellations are not always to be taken literally. *Bath brick* is really made at Bridgwater, *Windsor chairs* come mostly from Wycombe, only a small minority of *Brussels carpets*, not to mention *sprouts*, have ever been in Belgium, and *Panama* hats are made in South America. So also *Epsom salts, Seidlitz powder, Apollinaris water* describe ingredients originally derived only from places in Surrey,

Bohemia, and a spring near Remagen on the Rhine ; and *Portland cement* is named from resembling the colour of *Portland* (Dorset) *stone*.

Some words of this class are connected with less familiar localities. With *shillelagh*, the name of a wood in county Wicklow, cf. German *ziegenhainer*, a cudgel, from *Ziegenhain*, near Jena. Opening at random that admirable book Hobson-Jobson,[1] we find that *Dumdum*, famous for the expanding bullet, is the name of an arsenal near Calcutta, and that *dungaree*, coarse cotton cloth, is so called from one of the quarters of Bombay ; and further that the first word originally meant a mound and the second a hillock. *Rhubarb* is a corruption of *rha barbarum*, foreign *rha*, the drug named from the *Rha*, an old name of the Volga. In *bawbee* is commemorated the Scottish estate of *Sillebawby*, the laird of which was a 16th-century mint-master. The fur called *caracul*, somewhat resembling astrakhan, takes its name from *Qara-Qul*, i.e. black lake, near Bokhara—

> And on his head he placed his sheepskin cap,
> Black, glossy, curl'd, the fleece of Kara-Kul.
> (Matthew Arnold, Sohrab and Rustum.)

Moreover, the instinct which craves to explain the unfamiliar in terms of the familiar often leads to wrong associations of this kind. The *Tonquin bean*, formerly used for scenting snuff, is not Asiatic,

---

[1] A Glossary of Colloquial Anglo-Indian Words and Phrases, by Yule and Burnell. The title, the British soldier's version of the Mohammedan wailing-cry ' Ya Hasan ! Ya Hasan ! ' is a good example of that popular instinct for word-twisting which is often instrumental in giving a ' name ' appearance to the unintelligible.

but South American. It is properly *tonka bean*, from the native word used for it in Guiana. *Cayenne pepper*, which on the surface would appear to be a speciality of French Guiana, is a corruption of *kian*, a Brazilian word, and some of us are old enough to remember when *ki-an* was the educated pronunciation of the word. A bird belonging to the class of the *viduinae* is often called the *Whidah-bird*, from *Whidah*, in Dahomey, which is actually one of its habitats ; but this is an alteration of the much older *widow-bird*, translated from the Portuguese *viuva*, a nickname given by early Portuguese explorers because of the bird's black cap and trailing ' weeds '.

Another huge group of such words is supplied by the inventor or the popularizer. Although the horse-drawn vehicles which are now only of anti-quarian interest were not so infinitely differentiated as motor-cars, the old coach-builders showed some degree of inventiveness. The light two-wheeled *tilbury* was named from its designer,[1] the still more sporting *stanhope* was first built for *Fitzroy Stan-hope* (+ 1864), and *shillibeer*, originally an omnibus, but now a combined hearse and mourning-coach, was patented by *George Shillibeer*, who introduced London to the omnibus in 1829. Much older and more imaginative is the 18th-century *phaeton*, from the rash son (*Phaethōn*) of Helios, who tried unsuc-cessfully to drive his father's chariot. *Thomas*

[1] But the old slang *tilbury*, sixpence, was the fare paid to cross the Thames by the ferry at *Tilbury*. This is probably the origin of the slang *tizzy*, sixpence, as phonetic laws have no control over argotic formations ; cf. *swiz* for *swindle*.

Chippendale, a London cabinet-maker, published The Gentleman and Cabinet-Maker's Director in 1732, *Thomas Sheraton*, of the same craft, was the author of The Cabinet Maker and Upholsterer's Drawing-book (1791), and *Heppelwhite* was also an 18th-century designer of furniture. *Aldine* is from *Aldus Manutius*, a Venetian printer (+ 1515), the *Elzeviers*, whom we usually spell wrong, flourished in Holland (1592–1680), and *John Baskerville* (+ 1775) was a type-founder and printer at Birmingham. Most of the words mentioned in the preceding paragraph are commonly spelt with a small initial. One could go on taking examples from any other sphere of human activity, but it is more merciful to refrain.

Innumerable objects and devices have been named ornamentally from prominent figures of the age, e.g. the name of *Queen Victoria* is borne by a carriage, a gigantic water-lily (*Victoria regia*), a minor planet, a pigeon, a plum, a number of railway stations, an Australian province, and a whole crowd of modern settlements in various parts of the world. Now that there are no secrets left, it is unlikely that geographical nomenclature will receive further additions such as *Rhodesia*, from *Cecil Rhodes*, or the very fitting *Mount Everest*, from *Sir George Everest*, surveyor-general of India (+ 1866). The naming of newly discovered countries from explorers is a common phenomenon of the past, the biggest example being *America* from *Amerigo Vespucci*, of Florence, whose name was associated with the New World soon after 1500 ; but we have two curiously modern names given to mountain-ranges of the Old World.

One is our own *Pennine*, the invention of that ingenious forger of early 'chronicles', Charles Bertram (+ 1765), while the peaks of Southern Tirol which we call the *Dolomites* take their name from the double carbonate of lime and magnesia, which, in 1794, was christened *dolomite* in honour of the French geologist *Dolomieu*.

The *wellington boot,* recorded for 1817, no doubt suggested the later *blucher,* now, I fancy, obsolete. *Blucher* was also at one time used in London slang for non-privileged cabs which were allowed to pick up passengers at London stations after all the privileged cabs had been hired. The allusion is of course to the late arrival of *Blücher* at Waterloo. Similarly, in French, a 'retardataire' used to be called a *grouchy,* the name of the French marshal who failed to turn up to time on the same occasion. An overcoat without seams is still called a *raglan,* from the name of the British commander-in-chief during the Crimean War, and a 19th-century *Earl of Chesterfield* is commemorated in an overcoat and a couch. Sometimes such words are short-lived, e.g. *brodrick,* the new army cap introduced when *Mr. St. John Brodrick* (now Earl of Midleton) was Secretary for War (1900–3), *havelock,* a linen head-protection against the sun, from the Mutiny hero, and *nightingale,* a hospital bed-jacket.

Modern English seems to have given up this kind of word-creation. Perhaps our national heroes and celebrities are now too standardized for the purpose. One of the latest examples I can think of is the military belt called a *Sam Browne,* from *Sir Samuel*

Browne, V.C., a famous Anglo-Indian general of the later 19th century.

Then we have articles of attire named from their wearers. It seems to be generally agreed in the hatting trade that the *billycock* hat was first made for Thomas William Coke (+ 1842), generally known as *Billy Coke*, a member of a famous Norfolk family. It may be noted, however, that the Oxford Dictionary finds a hat described as ' bully-cocked ', i.e. worn in an aggressive manner, as early as 1712. The *billycock* of our youth was no more than the common *bowler*, which perpetuates the fame of a London hatter [1]—

Mr. Bowler, of 15 St. Swithin's Lane, has, by a very simple contrivance, invented a hat that is completely ventilated, whilst, at the same time, the head is relieved of the pressure experienced in wearing hats of the ordinary description (Daily News, Aug. 8, 1868).

The *Duc de Roquelaure* (+ 1738) brought a long cloak into fashion. The Scottish corruption *rokelay* is used of a woman's cloak. In German it became *rockelor*, and Schlegel was censured for the anachronism of using it to translate Shylock's ' gaberdine ' (Merchant of Venice, i. 3). More interesting is *Mrs. Gamp*, who habitually carried ' a species of gig-umbrella ' (Martin Chuzzlewit, ch. xix). The baggy umbrella is such an indispensable part of the comedian's equipment that it is not surprising to find French supplied with two words for *gamp*, viz. *riflard* and *pépin*, both from the names of characters

[1] I long regarded this as a fable, but have had to yield to evidence.

in French farces.[1] At one time *robinson* was used
in the same sense, from a comedy by Pixérécourt
(1805) in which *Robinson Crusoe* appeared with his
famous goat-skin parasol. With the *Gainsborough
hat* in which *Gainsborough* (+ 1788) loved to depict
his duchesses we may compare French *ferronnière*, a
jewelled ornament worn on the forehead, as in
Leonardo da Vinci's portrait of *La Belle Ferronnière*,
the fair ironmongress, mistress of Francis I.

So far all has been fairly plain-sailing, i.e. we
can put forward decisive or, at any rate, plausible
reasons for the selection of names.   The same applies
to names from history or myth, taken as types of
character, though the choice does not always seem
particularly apposite, e.g. the offence of *Ananias*
(Acts v.), the typical liar of history, did not go far
beyond the normal practice of the income-tax payer.
As for his opposite, *George Washington*, we have
only his own authority for the fact that he ' could
not tell a lie ', nor is there any satisfactory evidence
to show that he ever really tried.   The Observer
for April 8, 1832, referred to the death of Goethe,
' the venerable *Nestor* of European literature ', and
about the same time in 1932 every respectable
English newspaper, in recording the death of Lord
Harris, called him ' the *Nestor* of Cricket '.   Probably not five per cent of readers, at any rate in
1932, knew that *Nestor* was the oldest and sagest
of the Greek princes who set out to besiege Troy,
but no doubt they all felt that the right thing had
been said.   Will all future students of Miss Rebecca

[1] Picard, La Petite Ville (1801), and a vaudeville of 1806.

West, when they read, in The Judge, of ' that *Jane Cakebread* look that burned buildings have by daylight ', be aware that Jane was a poor old woman whose continual appearances as a ' drunk and disorderly ' made her a stock figure of the London police-courts ?

The real task that awaits a young and energetic philologist is the explanation, linguistic or psychological, of all the apparently arbitrary cases in which proper names are used as common nouns. We know that the Dutch *kop van Jut*, Jut's head, a strength-testing apparatus at fairs, is from the name of a notorious murderer, but we know not who was the original *Aunt Sally* of English fairs. Why should we distinguish the sex of the goat by the names *Billy* and *Nanny*, but that of the ass by *Jack* and *Jenny* ? Why should a cheap motor-car be called a *tin Lizzie* and an early musket a *brown Bess* ? Why should Satan bear such an extraordinary variety of names (pp. 68–71) ? We know that *bobby* and *peeler* come from *Robert Peel*, who created the modern London police force in 1829, having previously conferred a like benefit on Ireland, where the word *peeler* first came into use ; but why was the superseded watchman called a *Charley* ? Why should the first lieutenant be known to sailors as *Jimmy the one* and why should Portsmouth be called *Pompey* ? And, since we are among the sailors, who was *Davy Jones* ? Who first hoisted and named the *Jolly Roger*, why is the flag which announces departure called the *Blue Peter*, and who first called a petition from the crew, with the signatures so

arranged as not to show a ringleader, a *round robin* ?
When all these questions are answered, it still
remains to establish the historical origin of *Humpty-
Dumpty*, the precise locality of *Tom Tiddler's* [1]
ground, the family connections of *Jack Robinson*
and *Betty Martin*,[2] the original function of the
intensifying addition in the phrase ' like hell and
Tommy ', and of the same familiar name in *tommy-
rot*, and the identity of the gentleman whose lucid
explanation was first received with the appreciative
' I get you, *Steve* '.

The opposite process, the conversion of a common
noun into a proper name, is rare,[3] but we have a few
examples. *Islam* (related to *Moslem* and *Musulman*)
is an Arabic word for resignation. *Sikh*, Punjabi for
disciple, was applied especially to a sect established
in the 16th century by Nanak Shah, and has now
become a sort of national name. *Darazi* is Arabic for
a tailor (cf. *Darzee* the tailor-bird in the Jungle Book).
In the 11th century *Ismael al Darazi* founded in
Lebanon a sect which took from him the name
Duruz (pl.), now the tribe called *Druses*.

Finally, it may be observed that many words of
this kind come into existence in a very accidental
way. The naming of the *jacobin* pigeon from the
resemblance of its neck-feathers to a monk's cowl
is an example of a very common phenomenon, but
the *Jacobin friars* received that name from the
accident of the Parisian Dominicans establishing

[1] Also, in dialect, *Tittler, Tickler, Tinker*.

[2] ' All my eye and Betty Martin ' is found in the 18th century.

[3] i.e. in the special modern sense. As already sufficiently
shown, all proper names are made from significant words.

themselves near the church of *St. Jacques*. In 1789, their premises were seized by the most murder-ous section of the Revolutionary Party, since when a *Jacobin* has been a political ' ultra '. *Walpurgis-nacht*, May-day eve, suggests the witches' revel on the Brocken, but *Walpurga*, the English abbess of Heidenheim, had no connection with witches, her ' day ' being simply due to its being the date of the removal of her bones.

CHAPTER II

THE PUNNING INSTINCT

IN the process of converting the noun proper into the noun common we are often able to detect some historical reason, but, in the great majority of cases in which familiar names are given to types of character, animals, inanimate objects and all sorts of gadgets, we have to be satisfied with recording without explaining. Yet it is probable that at the back of many of these mysteries there lurks the spectre of folk-etymology, i.e. the popular fancy for giving the unfamiliar a more familiar aspect, or else an elementary pun [1]; and, as exemplified throughout this book, the proper name is the favourite medium for such linguistic antics. *Silly Billy* may have been suggested by rime and *Simple Simon* by alliteration. In a novel I have recently read an impecunious character describes himself as *Ben the beanless*, while Mr. P. G. Wodehouse is a little more elaborate with his *Pelham the pincher* for a plagiarist. A great number of familiar names are employed in this way, even unaccompanied by an adjective. The use of French *Guillaume* for a ' gull, dolt, fool ' (Cotgrave) is no doubt due to association with *guiller*, to beguile,

[1] See the examples from place-names (p. 151).

and *ninny*, pet-form of *Innocent*, is explicable, but
why should *Tony* have meant a simpleton since the
17th century ? And how did *dandy*, pet-form of
Andrew, acquire its present sense, which is 18th
century for the 17th-century *Jack-a-dandy* ? And
why should the same word mean, as we are informed
by the Oxford Dictionary, a sloop or cutter, with a
jigger-mast abaft, on which a mizzen-lug-sail is set ;
a piece of mechanism used for hoisting the trawl ;
a bantam fowl ; a small jug ; a running-out fire
for melting pig-iron in tin-plate manufacture ; a
small false grate fitted into a fireplace ; a light
iron hand-cart used to carry coke ; not to mention
*dandy-brush, dandy-cart, dandy-horse, dandy-line,
dandy-loom, dandy-roller* ? This list, infinitesimally
small compared with the chronicled activities of
Jack, will give some idea of this mysterious element
in our language. We find similar problems in all
the European languages, and, when we get into the
region of argot, the number of such applications of
familiar baptismal names becomes bewildering.

In Dorset a fool is called a *sammy*. This looks
like a special use of the name *Samuel*, but it is
nothing of the kind. Anglo-Saxon had a prefix
sam-, half, whence the epithet *sam-wis*, half-witted,
which survives in the Dorset surname Samways.
The type of intellect which the cockney describes as
' half-baked ' is in Dorset *sam-sodden*, i.e. half-
boiled, whence *sammy*, popularly assimilated to the
baptismal name. In the slang expression ' upon my
Sam ' we probably have a shortened form of *Salmon*,
i.e. *Salomon* or *Solomon*, described in early works on

slang as the ' beggars' oath '. *Sammy*, sometimes applied during the War to the American soldier, is of course from *Uncle Sam* (p. 158). The name *Robin* has a very large range of senses. The Old French *Jack* and *Jill* were *Robin* et *Marion*. Cotgrave, who had few illusions, renders ' Robin a trouvé Marion ' by ' a notorious knave hath found a notable queane '. The diminutive *robinet* means a water-tap, but *robin*, contemptuous for a lawyer (*homme de robe*), is an obvious pun, like *richard* for a plutocrat. We may compare the Middle English *robertsman*, a marauder, no doubt suggested by *rob*. *Colin*, a pet-form of *Nicholas*, became in both French and English a stock name for an operatic shepherd (e.g. Spenser's Colin Clout). We also have *Colin Maillard*, blind man's buff, and *Colin tampon*, the drum-beat of the Swiss guard, but *colin*, the coalfish, would seem to have been influenced by its Teutonic name. The name *Gerry* or *Jerry*, used during the War for *German*, was not due to any belief that Gerald or Jeremiah were favourite German names (cf. *Fritz* and *Heine*), but to the first syllable of the national adjective. Nor does a *Scotch and polly* (*apollinaris*) allude directly to a lady's name.

Some perversions are examples of elementary wit, e.g. the sailor's *Bully Ruffian* for *Bellerophon* and *Soup-tub* for *Superb*, or the British soldier's *pork and beans* for *Portuguese*. *Surajah Doula*, of Black Hole of Calcutta fame, was called by the British troops *Sir Roger Dowler*. So also we have the war-word *Minnie* for the German *minenwerfer*, mine-thrower, and *Nancy* for the American Naval Curtiss (*N.C.*) aeroplane, which belong to the same class of ideas as *Plug Street* for *Ploegstert* (plough-tail) wood. The Germans called their methods of whole-sale destruction in retreat *Alberich* (as though ' all break '), which means something like king of the elves (cf. the related Oberon, Old French Auberon). But *Archie*, an anti-aircraft gun, is an unexplained choice. The young airmen who trained at Brooklands before the War gave the name *Archibald* to an air-dis-turbance, which, prevailing regularly over the ground, was the cause of unpleasant air-bumps. The experi-ence of being shelled from the ground producing a very similar sensation, the name was transferred at the Front to the gun. The young officer who coined the name at Brooklands was killed early in the War, and the reason for his choice is unknown.[1] Proba-bly it was arbitrary. A young lady of my acquaint-ance, interested in entomology, is just now anxiously watching the development of a very fat chrysalis whom she calls *Cuthbert*,[2] and a stranded whale on exhibition at an East Anglian seaside resort is described as *Eric*.

An early example of the intrusion of the proper name is *Huguenot*. It is agreed among scholars that this is a corruption of *eiguenot*, a dialect form of German *eidgenoss*, confederate, ' oath-mate '. It

---

[1] This reads rather like one of the legends which I take pleasure in destroying, but the evidence is unimpeachable. See my Etymological Dictionary, s.v.

[2] The comic sense of this name (see p. 149) apparently dates from a pre-War music-hall song describing the adventures of three gilded youths, ' Cuthbert, Clarence and Claude.'

had at first a political significance and became
associated with Geneva when that city joined the
Swiss Confederation in 1518. The religious sense
was due to Geneva's being the rallying-point of
Continental protestantism. *Huguenet* and *Huguenot*
are Old French diminutives of *Hugues*, Hugh. It
is possible that the corruption was partly due to
association with a certain *Hugues* who was several
times mayor of Geneva and died in 1532, but it
is equally possible that the general instinct of folk-
etymology was responsible, and the basis of this
instinct is the desire to make the strange word look
or sound 'like something', this something being
most readily found in the form of some familiar
name.

In our dialects still linger such words as *benjamin*
(for *benzoin*) and *aaron lily*, familiar to the lexico-
graphers of the 17th century, who often convert the
lanner hawk into a *leonard*. So also the old-fashioned
cockney's *Solomon David* for *solemn affidavit*. A
good example is the Italian saying *Cesare o Niccolò*,
for 'Aut Caesar aut nihil', a motto attributed to
Caesar Borgia (+ 1507). In the same way the
Persian *attar of roses* becomes our vulgar *otto of
roses*, and the native name *budgerigar* of an Australian parakeet is altered to *beauregard*. The
Tudor writers described red hair as *Cain-coloured*
or *Judas-coloured*, this tint being considered sym-
bolical of the Biblical villain, but *Abram-coloured*
(Coriolanus, ii. 3), which seems to be of the same
class, is folk-etymology for *auburn*.

Though many names of plants (*ragged robin, sweet*

william, creeping jinny, prattling parnell, etc.) are actual nicknames, some of them are perversions of more scientific words, e.g. *cicely* or *cecily*, used of several umbelliferous plants, is the Greek *seseli*, and *sweet alison* is a corruption of the Latin *alyssum*.[1] Less graceful, but very characteristic of this tendency, is the Kent and Sussex *simpson*, groundsel, French *seneçon*, Latin *senecio*. *Tincture of Queen Anne* (quinine) is a good example of what folk-etymology can do in this direction, and I have even heard a rustic describe discursive remarks as *talking at Randall* (random). At Sheffield the *jolly wassail* of a Christmas song is actually altered to *Johnny Wesley*.

The spirit *gin* is shortened from *geneva*, an assimilation to a geographical name of the French *genièvre*, which is derived from *juniper*, with which gin is flavoured. In French dialect the plant sometimes becomes *geneviève*, the name of the patron saint of Paris. The organ-stop called a *cremona* is an alteration of German *krummhorn*, crooked horn, assisted by some hazy musical suggestion of *Cremona* as the home of Stradivari and Amati, the great violin-makers. Other perversions of the same type are *paduasoy*, as though silk from *Padua*, for Old French *pou de soie* (of unknown origin), and *mantua-maker*, a mistaken spelling of French *manteau*. The present-giving custom associated with a double kernel which we call *philippina* or *philopoena* comes from Germany, where *vielliebchen*, little darling, was

[1] From Greek *a-*, neg., and *lussa*, madness, from its supposed medicinal properties.

changed by folk-etymology into *philippchen*, little Philip. Forms of the word are found in several other European languages.

The origin of *maraud* is uncertain. The earliest trace we have of it is the French noun *maraud*, explained by Cotgrave as ' a rogue, begger, vagabond ; a varlet, rascall, scoundrell, base knave '. This is only recorded from the 15th century, while the proper name *Maraud*, from which I believe it was adopted by some obscure pun, is found in both French and English of the 12th century. However that may be, it was associated in the 17th century with the name of *Count Merode*, one of the most rapacious of the Imperialist commanders during the Thirty Years War. Some of the early etymologists, not knowing anything of the chronology of the word, derived it from the name of the Count, with the result that the corresponding Spanish verb is now *merodear*. French *gilet*, a waistcoat, was long regarded as a diminutive of *Gilles*, a clown (p. 2, n. 2), and a legend was evolved to connect the garment with an individual mountebank of the name. It is now recognized that, like the Spanish *gileco*, a slave's jerkin, it is of Turkish origin (*yelek*), having apparently been introduced into southern Europe, via Algiers, at a time when captivity among the Moors was no uncommon experience.

The etymology given by the Oxford Dictionary for *flamingo*, ' from the (flame) colour ', is incorrect, or at least inadequate. The French name is *flamant*, borrowed from the Provençal *flamenc*, the Spanish is *flamenco*, and the Portuguese is *flamengo*. All

c

these words mean *Fleming*,[1] and the bird was actually called a *fleming* also in English. It is impossible to say whether it was so named in allusion to the rich garb and florid appearance commonly attributed to the *Flemings* or whether in all the languages in which it occurs a sort of pun on *flame* was intended. At any rate, direct formation from *flame* is hardly possible by means of a suffix originally representing the Teutonic *-ing*.[2] *Jean de Gand* (John of Gaunt, Dutch *Gent*), a French name for the gannet, looks like another ' Fleming ', but is probably a play on *gent*, the Dutch name of the bird. In fact Dutch *de gent* means ' the gannet '.

These examples, taken at random, are meant to illustrate the fact that, numerous as are our words of personal name origin, one must always be on the look-out for some early pun and the primitive tendency to connect the common noun with some name. In French slang *Rébecca* is used of a lady fond of having the last word. This is not a reflection on the Biblical *Rebekah*,[3] whose surname, says Sir James Frazer, might very well have been *Sharp* (see Genesis, ch. xxvii), but a play on the verb *rebéquer*, to hold shrewishly to one's opinion, to ' peck back '. This suggests a digression on the ancient musical instrument called a *rebeck*, a kind

---

[1] *Flamant* is an archaic variant of Modern French *Flamand*.

[2] The parallel Old French *ferrant*, ? iron-grey, quoted by the Oxford Dictionary, is worthless. It is doubtful whether the word means more than simply steed, and it is probably of Arabic origin.

[3] For the *Rebecca rioters*, destroyers of toll-gates in South Wales (1843–4), see Genesis xxiv. 60.

of three-stringed fiddle. This was in medieval Latin *rebeca*, in Italian *ribeca*, in Portuguese *rebeca*. All these are perversions of a much earlier form found in Middle English as *ribibe* or *ribible*, in Old French as *rebebe*, and in archaic Italian as *ribebba*, all coming from Arabic *rebab*. This is the form used by Chaucer—

> Al konne he pleye on gyterne or ribible.
>
> (A. 4396.)

Now it is not phonetically possible for *ribib* to become *rebeck*, so we must assume the contortionist effects of folk-etymology, which seems to have been at work in the other languages also, the name of the instrument being assimilated for some reason to that of the mother of Jacob. Chaucer has the word *rebeck*, but it means an unpleasing old woman—

> ' Brother ', quod he, ' heere woneth an old rebekke
> That had almoost as lief to lese hir nekke
> As for to yeve a peny of hir good.'
>
> (D. 1573.)

In D. 1377 she is called ' an old wydewe, a *ribibe* ', showing the significant identity of the two words. From which I conclude, though the facts are rather confusing, that the Arabic word was altered in various languages by some mysterious association with the name *Rebecca*.

The proper name itself is naturally exposed to corruption. A Kentish long-shoreman with whom I forgathered as a schoolboy was deeply interested in the bringing to England of *Clara Patrick's needle*. *Bartholomew* for *Bath Oliver* (p. 9) I owe to a good little housemaid of unusual intelligence.

Cashmere, originally geographical, became in 18th-century English also *kerseymere*, by confusion with another fabric called *kersey*. In French it is *casimir*, an assimilation to a well-known name of Polish origin, and this passed into English as *cassimere*, still in use in the 19th century.

The corruption of the proper name into a common noun is unusual, but there are a few examples. The English *Aunt Sally* has become at French fairs *âne salé*, and the instrument of torture known as the *scavenger's daughter* takes its name from one *Skeffington*, governor of the Tower in the 16th century. This naturally suggests *darbies*, handcuffs, which is not a case of corruption. *Darby's bonds* seems to have been a 16th-century name for some sort of oppressive document popular with usurers—

> To make their coyne a net to catch young frie,
> To binde such babes in father Derbies bands.
>   (Gascoyne, Steel Glass.)

The sense of handcuffs is recorded in the 17th century, and the 18th-century *Johnny darbies* suggests that the personal name origin was still realized. *Darby's* identity is obscure, but he was certainly not the husband of *Joan*, as that loving pair are first mentioned in a song in the Gentleman's Magazine for 1735—

> Old Darby, with Joan by his side,
> You've often regarded with wonder :
> He's dropsical, she is sore-eyed,
> Yet they're never happy asunder.

CHAPTER III

FICTION AND MYTH

ALMOST every author or artist of any reputation has at some time or other had an adjective formed from his name. A recent Sunday
Times contained an allusion to the ' *Beardsleyesque*
moods and the *Ibsenites* of the nineties'. With the
historic *Dantesque, Shakespearean, Miltonic*, etc., we
may compare the more modern *Wellsian* and *Shavian*,
the latter formed from the name of *Mr. G. B. Shaw*
with the same phonetic substitution which we find
in *Harrovian*.[1] It is to be remarked that the two
most popular formations of this kind are connected
with representatives of the fantastic in literature.
Rabelaisian, from *François Rabelais* (+ 1553), connotes, according to the Oxford Dictionary, ' exuber-
ance of imagination and language, combined with
extravagance and coarseness of humour and satire '.
Gilbertian, from *W. S. Gilbert* (+ 1911), is used especially with ' situation ', to describe the kind of para-
doxical topsy-turvydom characteristic of the plots
of the Gilbert and Sullivan comic opera. Occasionally a famous book has given us an epithet, such as

---

[1] Cf. *Etonian, Rugbeian, Marlburian*, etc., but the product
of Winchester is a *Wykehamist*, from *William of Wykeham*, the
founder (1378).

Utopian, from Sir Thomas More's *Utopia* (1515–16), which, next to Robinson Crusoe, is probably the most ' European ' of all English literary works, and may be described as a Gilbertian fantasy written in serious mood. The modern *Ruritanian* (p. 152) is a parallel. With our *Euphuism*, an artificial style like that of Lyly in his *Euphues* (1578–80), cf. the less familiar *Gongorism* and *Marinism*, from the Spanish poet *Góngora* (+ 1627) and the Italian poet *Marini* (+ 1625).

The fact is that the human mind is especially susceptible to the odd and unusual.[1] The unkind assertion has even been made that Oxford produced only one work of genius in the 19th century—Alice in Wonderland ; and it has frequently been noticed that the only fictional character of modern times who has become a type and contributed to our vocabulary is *Sherlock Holmes*, with the pale shades of *Watson* and *Moriarty* in attendance ; and not all the skill of the great detective in classifying cigarette-ash or the characteristic muds of various counties would have made him a national figure without the assistance of his striking physique, his dressing-gown, violin, strong shag and hypodermic syringe, and his cruel delight in the imbecility of his *fidus Achates*.[2] In other words, Conan Doyle

[1] At present it seems particularly interested in the morally abnormal. It is difficult, in a modern highbrow novel, to escape the words *sadism* and *masochism*. The first, sensual delight in cruelty, is from *Comte* (commonly called *Marquis*) *de Sade* (+ 1814), author of infamous books ; the second, a kind of inverted sadism, from *Sacher Masoch* (+ 1895), an Austrian novelist.

[2] The faithful henchman of Aeneas.

went back to the methods of Dickens and Shakespeare, whose characters live to a great extent by their mannerisms. The fact that shocker-writers without number have striven less successfully to give a characteristic physiognomy to their own special detectives, amateur or professional, suggests that Conan Doyle had a touch of genius.

Victor Hugo, in his Préface de Cromwell, put forward the theory that modern art and literature differ from those of the ancients in the great part which the moderns allot to the grotesque. If we consider a few of the fictional characters which have become proverbial types and have lent themselves to the formation of adjectives and abstract nouns, we shall see that the grotesque dominates to a remarkable extent. It must also be admitted that the sinners are more popular than the saints. There is, for instance, hardly another character in fiction to equal the fame of *Don Juan*, the infidel and debauchee, a figure of Spanish legend introduced into literature by Tirso de Molina and popularized by Molière, Mozart, and Byron.

The word grotesque does not necessarily carry within it the implication of the ridiculous and contemptible. *Don Quixote*, the hero of the famous romance which all of us know and few of us have read, is one of the most grotesque characters in fiction, but Mr. Chesterton has recently written of 'the glorious insult of being called *quixotic*'. The adjective is defined by the Oxford Dictionary as 'striving with lofty enthusiasm for visionary ideals'. Cervantes died in 1616, but the adjective does not appear in English before the 19th century. To Cervantes we also owe *Dulcinea*, for an idealized and idolized mistress, and French *Maritorne*, a dirty and repellent wench. No characters of French literature have more firmly established themselves in language than the fantastic giants *Gargantua* and *Pantagruel* created by Rabelais (see p. 29), unless it be *Tartufe*, Molière's arch-hypocrite (1664) and his greatest achievement in the more serious grotesque. To Molière French also owes the use of *Agnès* for a demurely artful *ingénue* (École des Femmes), the name having been previously in general French use for a simpleton.

Italian has given us *rodomontade*, recorded c. 1600, from *Rodomont*,[1] a bragging Saracen leader in Ariosto's Orlando Furioso. About the same time Spenser, under Italian influence, coined *Braggadocio*, as the personification of vainglory. A much later creation of the same type is *Bombastes Furioso*, a mock-epic (1815) by W. B. Rhodes, the name being suggested by *bombast*, originally cotton-wool used for padding, but recorded as early as the 16th century in the sense of inflated or turgid language. To the Italians also we owe *pander*, noun and verb, for it was from Boccaccio that Chaucer took the story of the traditional rôle of *Pandarus* as go-between in the amours of Troilus and Cressida—

If ever you prove false one to another, since I have taken such pains to bring you together, let all pitiful goers between be called to the world's end after my name : call them all Panders.

(Shakespeare, Troilus and Cressida, iii. 2.)

---

[1] The name *Rodamonte* was originally coined by Boiardo. It means ' roll-mountain ' and is of the *Shake-spear* type.

We now use *pander* mostly as a verb, as in the alliterative masterpiece of an English judge (Mr. Justice Avory, Dec. 17, 1920), who condemned 'The pernicious practice which prevails of pandering to the prurient proclivities of the public by publishing pictorially the lurid details, etc.'

When we come to Shakespeare, the appeal of the grotesque is unmistakable, as also the general fact that in all literature it is not heroes and heroines who become proverbial, but the subordinate oddities, i.e. the 'characters'. Such are *Shylock*, often used for usurer,[1] in some ways an exception to the above rule, for he is the hero of the play and, according to Heine, its only decent male character; *Dogberry*, the foolish constable of Much Ado about Nothing, whence *Dogberrydom*, approximating in sense to the later *Bumbledom*; *Falstaff*, and the super-grotesque *Caliban*, 'savage and deformed slave', in whom Shakespeare personified the bestial impulses which are always threatening to wreck the fabric of ordered society. The name *Autolycus* calls up to us Shakespeare's 'snapper-up of unconsidered trifles' (Winter's Tale, iv. 3) rather than the son of Mercury and arch-thief of ancient myth whom Shakespeare borrowed for his play. All the above names come, as is natural, from the comedies, whence also *Ariel*, 'an airy spirit', most appropriately used by M. André Maurois for his romanticized life of Shelley, and *Portia*, which is good journalese for a lady barrister.

[1] 'Blood-sucking Shylock' is now good 'Labour' English for any thrifty individual who invests his modest savings.

Shakespearean characters are familiar to us all, but some names which have had remarkable success in language come from authors and works long forgotten. A good example is *Mrs. Grundy*, from Tom Morton's rural comedy Speed the Plough (1798), in which Dame Ashfield, a farmer's wife, is always irritating her husband with her anxious ' What will Mrs. Grundy say ? ' To this forgotten writer we also owe the usually misquoted ' Approbation from Sir Hubert Stanley is praise indeed '. His son, Madison Morton, was the author of the famous farce *Box and Cox* (1847), sometimes used allusively of a bedroom made to accommodate two occupants at different times. For *Jeremy Diddler* see p. 107. *Lothario*, usually described as ' gay ', owes his fame to his rôle as lady-killer in Rowe's Fair Penitent (1703)—

Is this that haughty gallant, gay Lothario ?

(v. 1),

though the name had already been used for a similar character in Davenant's Cruel Brother (1630).

Philander, which we now use only as a verb, is a lover in more than one Italian romance, but the popularity of the name in English seems to date from 17th-century love-ballads about *Philander* and *Phyllis*. The name is due to a misunderstanding, the Greek *philandros*, lover of man, conjugally affectionate, being an adjective properly applied to women. *Phyllis*, it may be remarked, is the name of a typical country maiden, but, via Milton's ' neat-handed Phillis ' (Allegro), has become conventional for a waitress. In old numbers of Punch the sentimental young pair are usually *Edwin* and *Angelina*, from Goldsmith's ballad, ' Turn, gentle hermit of the dale '. The *real Simon Pure* is the name of a Quaker in Mrs. Centlivre's Bold Stroke for a Wife (1717), who, in part of the play, is impersonated by another character. *Frankenstein* was a student, who, in Mrs. Shelley's story of that name (1818), created a monster which he could not control. By a popular confusion of ideas he is often misused for the monster. One of the latest names to come into similar use is *Pooh-Bah*, ' Lord High Everything Else ', in Gilbert's Mikado, and now current English for a pluralist holder of public offices. Latest of all is probably *Felix the cat*, a product of the films.

It was not until the 19th century that the English novel began to supply the language with typical characters. It is true that the 18th-century *Lovelace*, in Clarissa Harlowe, has been occasionally used for a debauchee, but this is much commoner in France, where Richardson had a tremendous vogue. On the other hand we have borrowed from France *Pangloss*, the incurable optimist in Voltaire's Candide (1759), convinced that ' tout est pour le mieux dans le meilleur des mondes possibles '. Perhaps France's most European word of this type is *Chauvin*, the French ' jingo ', an old grenadier of Rochefort, who was introduced into several plays and popular songs of the 19th century. It was via a French translation that we first became acquainted with the Arabian Nights, to which we owe *Alnaschar dreams*, the castles in the air built by the barber's fifth brother, and *Barmecide banquet*, an imaginary feast such as that offered to a beggar by one of that famous family. *Collins*, a letter of thanks written after a stay with friends, is from the egregious *Mr. Collins* of Jane Austen's Pride and Prejudice (1813), but this application of the name is, I believe, quite modern. Scott created a gallery of ' characters ' unequalled except by Shakespeare and Dickens, but the only contribution they have made to language is the name of the *Dandie Dinmont* terrier, from the stalwart Borderer in Guy Mannering.

Dickens best illustrates the opinion with which this chapter starts, viz. that what appeals to mankind is not so much the exact portrayal of average human nature, which is really not very interesting, as that oddity of character which the eye of genius is quick to notice and the pen of genius to depict. A distinguished French critic, Edmond Scherer, complains—

' Cet habile romancier excelle à modeler une physonomie risible ou repoussante, à appliquer ce masque sur un mannequin dont le costume ne sera pas moins bizarre, puis à prêter au héros ainsi fait quelque redite burlesque, quelque repartie humoristique laquelle, jetée à travers les scènes les plus diverses, produit un certain comique de bas aloi. Les êtres ainsi créés sont frappants, ils sont reconnaissables, mais ils ne vivent pas.'

Too true, alas ! One seems to remember something of the same kind in Shakespeare. Is there not a lack of variety in the wording of Corporal Nym's philosophic comments ? One of the acutest of our own younger critics puts it, to my mind, more reasonably, when he speaks of Dickens as ' the high-spirited magician who could condense the absurdities of a score of human beings into one perfect character in fiction '. It may be surmised that the author of this book is an unrepentant Dickensian.

I have been told by many bright young people that they ' cannot read Dickens ', so this paragraph, superfluous to the literate, is for the information of the aforesaid young people. For ' in a *Pickwickian sense* ', the Oxford Dictionary gives the luminous explanation, ' in a technical, constructive, or conveniently idiosyncratic or esoteric sense '. The same authority registers *Welleresque, Wellerian,* and *Wellerism* as words descriptive of the linguistic style affected by *Sam Weller*. *Stiggins* is equivalent to a hypocritically puritanical kill-joy. *Bumble*, the beadle in Oliver Twist, is perpetuated in *bumbledom*, a name for the baser type of bureaucracy, and *Sikes* is good English for a burglar. *Squeers* is a brutal type of schoolmaster, now presumably extinct, and *Vincent Crummles*, whom Nicholas Nickleby joined after leaving Dotheboys Hall, is a symbol of the old type of strolling actor. A book on the older stage, published last year, had the title When Crummles Played. *Pecksniff* was the arch-humbug in Martin Chuzzlewit. The same novel gave us the immortal *Sairey Gamp* and her spectral invention, *Mrs. Harris*. *Chadband*, in Bleak House, is a kind of non-alcoholic *Stiggins*, and *Podsnap*, in Our Mutual Friend, the incarnation of complacent British philistinism, with a trick of ' waving aside ' all objections. The aged can remember when *Dolly Varden* frocks and patterns, from the charming daughter of the old locksmith in Barnaby Rudge, were still popular. *Micawber*, in David Copperfield, is the type of man

who hopes optimistically for 'something to turn
up'. In 1909 Mr. Robert Blatchford wrote pro-
phetically, 'It is not safe to trust the tradition of
Micawber against the tradition of blood and iron.'

The above are examples of names which have so
far become an essential part of educated English
as to form derivatives, e.g. *Micawberism* or *Peck-
sniffian*, the latter ruled 'out of order' by the
Speaker in April, 1928, but one could enumerate
from the same source scores of others which are
almost equally familiar to the well-read. A pair
of good Dickensians arriving in Glasgow on a wet
Sunday would almost inevitably brace each other
with a reminder of *Mark Tapley*, and, if one of
them weakened, he might reasonably expect a mur-
mured admonition against *Gummidging*. Even characters who have almost silent parts are remembered.
In one of her novels, Mary Cholmondeley remarks
on the futility of arguing with people who can
'make a *Jorkins* of the Almighty'. Now, who was
Jorkins [1] ?

If we take a long stride back into remotest antiquity, we find that it is still the representatives of
the strange and deformed which supply us with
expressive words. *Cerberus*, the canine doorkeeper
of Hades, whose vigilance had to be lulled by a

---

[1] Dickensians will not need to be reminded that he was
Mr. Spenlow's almost invisible partner (see David Copperfield,
ch. xxxviii). In a book on London topography, which contains
numerous references to Dickens, I find an allusion to ' The spring
bath in which David Copperfield used to go for a cooler when
he was engaged to Dora Spenlove, Betty Trotwood's niece.'
We all make occasional slips, but really !

' sop ', had three heads. *Briareus* had a hundred hands and *Argus* a hundred eyes, which, after his death, were transferred to the peacock's tail—

> He is a gouty Briareus, many hands and no use ; or a pur-blinded Argus, all eyes and no sight.
>
> (Troilus and Cressida, i. 2.)

Polyphemus,[1] on the other hand, like the rest of the *Cyclopes* (i.e. circle-eyes) had but one. According to the Century Dictionary *polyphemous* means ' monoculous ', and many elderly professors of Romance philology scattered about Europe will remember how the formidable monocle of the greatest of French philologists earned for him the affectionate nickname *Polyphème*. The *harpies*, i.e. clutchers, are described by Hesiod as winged maidens, but we picture them rather in their later form of hideous creatures with haggard faces and long claws. Of the twelve *labours of Hercules* we remember best his encounter with the *hydra* [2] (i.e. water-snake) of Lerna, whose nine heads grew again as fast as they were struck off.

We are curiously selective when we use as types figures from myth, the most ancient form of fiction. Of the three Graces we know best

> That goddess fair and free,
> In Heaven yclept *Euphrosyne*.
>
> (Allegro.)

Of the three judges of the underworld we know only *Rhadamanthus*. *Rhadamanthine* is good English

[1] Lit. ' many-voiced '.
[2] Though the cleansing of the stables of *Augeas*, King of Elis, is an indispensable metaphor for the reformer.

for judicially severe, and on May 15, 1923, H. H.
Asquith (as he then was) described T. P. O'Connor,
censor of cinemas, as the ' *Rhadamanthus* of the
film world '. Of the three Fates *Atropos*, i.e. the
inflexible, whom Milton, in a forgetful moment,
calls ' the blind Fury with the abhorred shears ',
has given her name to a poisonous alkaloid. We
sometimes refer to the *Furies* or *Eumenides*,[1] but
not by name, though one of them, *Megaera*, has
supplied French with a word meaning virago. *La
mégère apprivoisée* is the usual French rendering of
the Taming of the Shrew. Of the nine Muses we
have chosen the least intellectual; ' devotee of the
Terpsichorean art ' is indispensable for a keen
dancer. Of the *Gorgons*, i.e. terrible ones, our
favourite is *Medusa*, whose name was given by
Linnaeus to a genus of jelly-fish with tentacles
suggesting snaky locks.

The fantastic wanderings of Ulysses, the em-
bodiment of Greek sagacity, have made a much
larger contribution to popular speech than the
heroic adventure of the Iliad. We speak of *Cim-
merian darkness*, from the *Cimmerii*, who, according to Homer, dwelt on the ocean in perpetual
mists, of *Circe's cup*, from the island enchantress
whose potion turned the wanderer's companions
into swine, of the *sirens*,[2] whose song Ulysses
managed ingeniously to hear without risk, of *Scylla*

[1] A propitiatory substitution (= well-intentioned) for the
older *Erinyes*.

[2] They also tried to allure the *Argonauts*, who sailed with
Jason in the *Argos* in quest of the Golden Fleece, but Orpheus,
who was on board, outsang them.

and *Charybdis*, two rocks[1] between Italy and Sicily, which were the ' frying-pan ' and the ' fire ' of the ancient world, and of his faithful wife *Penelope*, who wove her ' web ' during the day and unravelled it at night, having promised to ' presume ' the death of Ulysses and take a new mate when it was finished. It is also from the Odyssean account of Hades that we take our idea of *Tantalus* (p. 6) and of *Sisyphus*, condemned eternally to roll up-hill a stone which always rolled down again. With *Sisyphean* toil, labour, etc., we may compare *Danaïdan* task, from the punishment of the fifty daughters of the Argive King *Danaus*, who, for the murder of their husbands, were doomed for ever in Hades to draw water in sieves. Even in the story of Troy possibly the most familiar incident lending itself to allusion is the rather grotesque affair of the wooden horse, the *Greek gift*.

Among the gods it is not Zeus or Hera, but *Hermes*, the Olympian Pooh-bah, thief, inventor, herald, messenger, go-between, dicer, gymnast, trader and general artful dodger of ancient myth, who has done most for the dictionary. As *Hermes Trismegistos*, i.e. thrice-greatest, he was worshipped by early mystics and alchemists, *hermetic* being used both of the occult and the air-tight. His name gave to Christian theology the science of *hermeneutics*, i.e. interpretation. By *Aphrodite* he had a son *Hermaphroditus*, in whom the sexes were united. He is more familiar to us by his Latin name *Mercury*. And here it may be noted that we usually speak

[1] According to some authorities *Charybdis* was a whirlpool.

of the gods and goddesses by their Latin rather than their Greek names.[1] *Eros* and his mother *Aphrodite*, to whom we owe *erotic* and *aphrodisiac*, are less familiar to us than *Cupid* and *Venus*. *Vulcan*, whence *vulcanite*, is more familiar than *Hephaestus*, and *Mars* than *Ares*. The Authorized Version renders the Greek *Areopagus* by *Mars' Hill* (Acts xvii. 22). A learned lady is a *Minerva* rather than an *Athene* or a *Pallas*,[2] though the *palladium*, the image of *Pallas* at Troy, has long been familiar in the sense of a national safeguard.

Those born under the planet *Mercury* are said to be *mercurial*, as others are *martial*, *saturnine* or *jovial*. The sense we give to the adjective is partly due to the god's name having been given to quicksilver. *Mercury* is used in most European countries for a newspaper, and has also made a large contribution to botanical nomenclature.

Euhemerus of Sicily put forward, c. 316 B.C., the theory that the gods of Greece were originally national heroes, later deified. This theory is called *euhemerism*. The modern view is rather that they represent personifications of natural forces, like the northern *Thor*, the thunder-god, given human form and attributes by the instinct known as anthropomorphism, an instinct

[1] This is putting it roughly, as the Roman divinities sometimes correspond only vaguely to the Greek divinities with which they were identified.

[2] *Palladian* architecture is from the Italian *Andrea Palladio* + 1580).

which persists in the creation of more modern types—

Pierrot [1] et Polichinelle [1] contiennent autant d'anthropomorphisme divin qu'en peuvent concevoir des cerveaux à peine formés et déjà terriblement actifs. Ils sont l'Hermès et le Zeus de nos bébés.

(Anatole France.)

The purpose of this digression on the mythology of the ancients is to illustrate the thesis with which we began, viz. the fact that it is usually the more fantastic character that impresses the human mind. The ancients are rather out of fashion now, and what were once commonplace allusions to early myth often require elucidation. A high authority on the science and art of advertising has lately delivered himself of the great truth that ' the classics are no good '. That being the case, evidently the classics must go. At the same time it must be remembered that English literature, almost up to date, is saturated with classical allusions, and that not only Shakespeare, Milton and Keats, but even Mr. Wells, will not always be perfectly intelligible, if the classics are to be banned. When the last-named writer likens (in Mr. Polly) the excited ironmonger entangled in a collection of rubber hose to *Laocoon*, he is permitting himself

---

[1] *Pierrot*, the white-faced, white-garbed, seems to be a late French addition to the Italian *commedia* (see p. 74, n.1). Besides meaning sparrow, the name is used, like our *Jack* and Spanish *Pedro*, for a humble servitor. The flockmaster, in La Fontaine, who lost his money, was reduced to acting as shepherd—

Celui qui s'était vu Coridon ou Tircis
Fut Pierrot, et rien davantage.

Polichinelle, whence our *Punchinello*, is of Italian origin.

an allusion which may to the next generation be a *Delphic utterance.*

The nomenclature of astronomy was created from Greek mythology at a time when our own ancestors lived in burrows. The alchemist followed suit, and not only the modern astronomer and chemist, but the geologist, botanist and zoologist, have continued to load our language with what Mr. Sinclair Lewis has somewhere called this ' universal scientific Hellenistic jargon ', which, after all, for international purposes, is a very useful and practical jargon. Anything liable to constant change is connected by the biologist with *Proteus,* the elusive sea-god, the botanist or chemist who wants a new word relating to the properties of the orange at once appeals to the *Hesperides,* the guardians of the golden apples in the west, and a zoologist in search of new names for two South American monkeys actually took *Rhesus* and *Entellus* from the Aeneid. *Python,* the huge snake sprung from the mud of Deucalion's flood and slain by Apollo near Delphi, was adopted early in the 19th century as a name for super-serpents. Geologists describe formations as *Neptunian* or *Plutonic,* i.e. due to water or fire, and the *Achilles tendon* is an allusion to the vulnerable heel by which his mother held him when she dipped him in the Styx. *Atlas,* i.e. the bearer, the Titan who bore the world on his shoulders, gave his name to a range of African mountains and to the adjacent ocean. When Kremer, the 16th-century Flemish geographer who latinized himself as *Mercator,* used the Titan's figure as the frontispiece of his volume

of maps, he gave us the common noun *atlas*. The
same figure suggested to Matthew Arnold the
weary Titan as a symbol of Britain. Even so
modern a person as the psycho-analyst cannot get
along without the *Oedipus complex*, for an incestuous
affection, or *Narcissism*, for morbid self-admiration,
such as that which resulted in *Narcissus* being
changed into a flower.

Up to quite recent times all ' respectable ' people
had some tincture of ancient mythology. Miss Tox,
it will be remembered, was always ready with an
apposite allusion—

' I do not think, I will tell you candidly, that Wickham is a
person of very cheerful spirit, or what one would call a——'
' A daughter of Momus,' Miss Tox softly suggested.

(Dombey and Son, ch. viii.),

and even Dickens's humbler characters knew, somewhat vaguely, the figures of the ' youth of the world ' ;
Mr. Weller, senior, disapproved of ' calling a young
ooman a *Wenus* ', Mrs. Dowler's chairman, unable
to obtain admission into her house in Royal Crescent,
Bath, opined, ' Servants is in the arms of *Porpus* ',
and Mrs. Joe Gargery, forsaking myth for history,
was firmly determined that Pip should not be
pompeyed.

CHAPTER IV

GADGETS

AN infinite number of objects bear names which can be historically connected with makers or inventors. This goes back to antiquity, an early example being the *Archimedean screw*, for raising water, which was invented by that mathematician of Syracuse (3rd century B.C.), who, discovering in his bath the principle of specific gravity, was apparently so excited as to drop an aspirate and cry *eureka !* [1] Less ancient, but still of respectable antiquity, is French *batiste*, cambric, from the name of a 13th-century weaver of Cambrai (Flemish Kamerijk). A venerable superstition connects our *blanket* with a 14th-century *Thomas Blanket* of Bristol, but the word is a Norman-French translation of the Anglo-Saxon *hwitel*, from *hwit*, white, whence the synonymous dialect *whittle*. If *Thomas Blanket* actually manufactured the article in question, he was named from his wares, like the ancestors of Messrs. *Whitbread, Goodbeer, Sowerbutts*, etc. Another *whittle*, a knife, earlier *thwitel* (from Anglo-Saxon *thwitan*, to cut), was associated with Sheffield as early as the 14th

[1] For *heurēka*, perfect of *heuriskein*, to find.

46

century.   We are told of the Miller of Trumping-
ton—

> A Sheffield thwitel baar he in his hose.
>
> (Chaucer, A. 3933.)

Whether an early cutler's name is contained in the
Scottish *jockteleg*, a clasp-knife, is doubtful.   Lord
Hailes wrote (c. 1776), ' The etymology of this word
remained unknown till not many years ago an old
knife was found having this inscription : Jacques de
Liège, the name of the cutler '.   It is regrettable
that the ' old knife ' was not at once deposited in
the national archives.   If, however, this *Jacques*
is a fact, we may compare French *eustache*, the
trusted weapon of the Parisian apache, which takes
its name from *Eustache Dubois*, an 18th-century
cutler of Saint-Étienne.   A corruption of *jockteleg*
is *jackleg*, which may have suggested the later *jack-
knife*.   The *bowie* was popularized by *Colonel Bowie*
(+ 1836)—

> He smiled—a bitter smile to see,—
> And drew the weapon of Bowie.
>
> (Bret Harte, A Moral Vindicator),

and the *colt* bears the name of another American
colonel, who also (in 1835) coined the word *revolver*.
Rather later is the *derringer*, likewise from the
inventor's name.

So long as the inventor and his gadget are linked
in speech, the name has hardly undergone the
transition with which this book deals.   Examples
are the *Torricellian experiment* (whence the baro-
meter), from *Torricelli*, the Italian physicist (+ 1647),
or the *Yale lock*, from a 19th-century American

inventor. In anatomy and surgery we have the *Eustachian tubes*, from the Italian anatomist *Eustachius* (+ 1574), and the *Taliacotian operation*, or nose-reconstruction, from *Tagliacozzi*, a surgeon of Bologna (+ 1599).

It is when the individual disappears behind the invention or new idea and sheds the capital letter that he becomes etymologically interesting, as in the contemporary *marcelled* hair, from the name of a Parisian coiffeur, and the more ancient *sally lunn*, from the young woman who cried this delicacy at Bath c. 1780–90, *tompion*, a watch or clock by *Thomas Tompion* (temp. Anne), or *pinchbeck*, an alloy invented by *Christopher Pinchbeck*, a Fleet Street watch-maker (+ 1732). The latter word is now usually figurative, like *brummagem* [1], e.g. it was applied by Mr. Lansbury as an epithet to the National Government in March, 1932. *Bloomers* seem to be coming in again, the word not the garment. This takes its name from *Mrs. Bloomer* (+ 1894), an American advocate of rational dress 'who introduced the costume' (Oxford Dictionary) ; but, according to Thornton's American Glossary, 'she did not invent it, was not the first to wear it, and protested against it being called by her name.' Charnock's [2] 'first set on *foot* (my italics!) by Mrs. Bloomer' seems to be true Victorian delicacy. *Tam o' shanter* and *trilby* (hat) are of literary provenience (Burns and George du Maurier). With *silhouette*, named in derision of the French

---

[1] The original allusion (17th century) was to counterfeit coins made at *Birmingham*.   [2] See p. 169, n. 1.

politician *Étienne de Silhouette* (+ 1767), we may
compare the more modern *poubelle*, a dust-bin, from
the name of a Prefect of the Seine under whose
rule it was introduced.   When, on October 10, 1789,
Dr. Guillotin proposed in the Assembly the introduction of a more merciful instrument of capital
punishment, the mechanical details of the device
were left to a *Dr. Louis*, with the result that it
was long called a *louisette* or *louison*, and also, for
some mysterious reason, was affectionately named
Marianne.   A humbler humanitarian than *Guillotin*
was the Surinam negro *Quassi*, who first discovered
the curative qualities of a plant which Linnaeus
honoured him by naming *quassia*.   We may compare *matico*, i.e. little Matthew, said to be so called
from a Spanish soldier who discovered the styptic
virtues of this South American herb.   What we
now call grape-fruit was formerly *shaddock*, from
a *Captain Shaddock* who introduced it into the West
Indies from the East Indies.   *Bramley*, of the
' seedling ', was a butcher at Southwell, Notts, and
the *William pear* was called by a Hammersmith
gardener *Williams' bon chrétien*.   The French name
is said to have been given in honour of St. François
de Sales (16th century).   The *gentian* was, according to Pliny, named from *Gentius*, King of Illyria
(2nd century B.C.), who discovered its properties.
Nearly all our flower-names in *-ia* are named from
botanists or celebrities, e.g. the *gardenia* from *Dr.
A. Garden*, Vice-president of the Royal Society
(+ 1791).

Then we have the scientific men, *Galvani* and

Volta, Italian physicists (+ 1792, 1827), *Mesmer*, an Austrian physician (+ 1815), and a whole series of electrical experts who have given their names to various ' units ', e.g. after *volt(a)*, we have *ohm*, *amp(ère)*, *farad(ay)*, *joule*, *watt*, *coulomb*. A representative of actuarial science was the Neapolitan banker *Lorenzo Tonti*, who, in 1653, put before Mazarin a scheme of insurance by which—

a number of sprightly youths (the more the merrier) put up a certain sum of money, which is then funded in a pool under trustees ; coming on for a century later, the proceeds are fluttered for a moment in the face of the last survivor, who is probably deaf, so that he cannot even hear of his success—and who is certainly dying, so that he might just as well have lost.
(Stevenson, The Wrong Box.)

Still further back dates the word *algorism*, archaic for arithmetic, which is derived from *Al-Khwarazmi*, i.e. the man of *Khwarazam* (Khiva), the surname of a celebrated Arab mathematician of the 9th century whose treatises made the Arabic decimal system known to Europe. The French form *algorithme* is due to association with Greek *arithmos*, number.

The preceding paragraphs might be multiplied by a hundred without exhausting the subject, but it is time to turn to another phenomenon, viz. the way in which nicknames are applied to all sorts of objects, implements and devices [1] in what seems, as a rule, quite arbitrary fashion. The obsolete fourpenny-piece is believed to have been called a *joey* after *Joseph Hume* (+ 1855), the economist, who advocated its introduction, but the *bob* is a mystery. The obsolete *joseph*, a long riding-

[1] Cf. *dandy* (p. 20).

cloak of the 17th century, was perhaps a witticism suggested by *Joseph's* ' coat of many colours ' (Genesis xxxvii. 3) or by the garment he left in the clutch of Potiphar's wife (Genesis xxxix. 12). If so, the later *benjamin*, a coachman's overcoat, was probably a playful variation on the same theme. The nautical *davit* may be due to the occasion when *David* was let down from a window (1 Samuel xix. 12), just as the legend of *Davy Jones* may go back to some rather confused version of the story of *Jonah*, formerly *Jonas*. The great example is *jack*, which, besides its numberless applications to humans, animals, plants, etc., is the name of a score of pieces of mechanism or devices for dispensing with labour. In this special sense the ultimate allusion is no doubt to *Jack*, the humble employee, e.g. *bootjack* is in German *stiefelknecht*, i.e. boot-varlet. As the name of a defensive coat (whence the diminutive *jacket*) and also of a leathern drinking-vessel (*black jack*), it comes immediately from Old French *jacques* with the same meanings.

Jenny, in *spinning-jenny*, is said to have been the name of Arkwright's wife. It is much more likely that the name was taken at random, like *betty*, formerly used of the burglar's *jemmy*, or *peggy* and *dolly*, both combined with ' tub ' in the north to describe a laundry apparatus. Anyhow there is no clue in the way of conjugal admiration to explain why a locomotive crane, a special type of compasses, and an ' in off ' at billiards (long or short) should also be called *jenny*. In this region of word-lore one has to be satisfied with noting without attempting to solve such problems as why elastic-side boots are called *jemimas* or why the French poilu calls the 75-millimetre gun *Joséphine* and his bayonet *Rosalie*. Of the latter, however, a fairly plausible explanation has been given, viz. that *Rosalie* is in France a stock name for a ' bonne à tout faire ', and that the bayonet is much more often used as a screwdriver, toasting-fork, etc., than for its legitimate purpose of exploring the foeman's anatomy.

When surnames are used in this way we can follow them a little further. The word *greenacre*, used by London stevedores when a set of goods falls out of the slings, must surely be a witticism connected with *James Greenacre*,[1] hanged for murder in 1837. An executioner who flourished c. 1600 is commemorated in the hoisting apparatus called a *derrick*, and we have the numerous articles named in honour of celebrities, such as the *brougham* from *Lord Brougham* (+ 1868), or the various colours, fashions, etc., which are connected with the name of Louis XV.'s mistress *Madame de Pompadour*. Some words even of this type are not very transparent. It is easy to connect the *cardigan* with the nobleman who led the charge of the Light Brigade, but no one has yet discovered what the *Duke of Alva*, tyrant of the Netherlands (16th century), has to do with the Dutch word *dukdalf*, pile-work to which ships are moored.

It has been observed by a French poet that the

---

[1] He is in the D.N.B., which, by a disastrous oversight, omits Charles Peace from our national celebrities.

spirit of mechanical progress is always accompanied by an attendant ape.[1] The one is intent on applying knowledge to the alleviation of man's sorry lot on earth, the other on discovering more efficient means of smashing human bones and lacerating human tissues. In a notorious murder trial a few years ago an eminent representative of Scotland Yard stated that he did not know what was meant by a *gat*. This confirms the opinion that the Yard does not read Edgar Wallace. *Gat* is short for *gatling*, a machine-gun invented by *Dr. R. J. Gatling* and first used in the American Civil War. Its use for the historic *colt* and *derringer*, or the ' ugly snub-nosed automatic ' of modern fiction, seems to be due to the American predilection for words which exaggerate size. Thus the pistol becomes a *gun* [2] and its bearer a *gunman*, a type which seems to flourish most luxuriantly in free republics and in countries that have aspirations that way.

The great gun seems, by its size, noise and general impressiveness, to have assumed for our ancestors a sort of human character resulting in the attribution of a personal name. Let us work backwards. The giant gun which, during the War, dropped shells into Paris from a distance of about seventy miles, was affectionately called by the Germans *die dicke* (fat) *Bertha*, from the name of the lady

[1]   Un ménechme hideux, son singe et son bouffon . . .
       En fait l'ignoble parodie.

                              (Théodore de Banville.)
[2] The Oxford Dictionary does not record this sense, defining the later sense of *gun* as ' any handgun except the pistol ', but the use is fairly old in the States.

who inherited the Krupp works and millions. About the same period a 6-inch howitzer collecting War Loan subscriptions in the East End of London was greeted as *Hungry Liz*. At the siege of Ladysmith our garrison was much annoyed by a Boer cannon known as *Long Tom*,[1] which had long been a name in the British Navy for a gun of great range and calibre. During the Royalist uprising of the Vendeans (1793) at the time of the French Revolution the peasants regarded as a sort of mascot one *Marie-Jeanne*, an antiquated field-piece which they dragged about everywhere with them. At Edinburgh castle is a 15th-century culverin known as *Long Meg*, from its size, or *Mons Meg*, from the Belgian town where it was probably cast. A German gun famous in the Brandenburg wars of the early 15th century was called *die faule Grete*, lazy Peg.

With the 14th century we come to the mother of guns, i.e. the *Lady Gunhilda*. Like *artillery*, originally used of bows and arrows, the word *gun* is pre-gunpowder. The first mention is dated 1339, when ' sex instrumenta de latone (brass) vocitata gonnes ' are included in an inventory of the London Guildhall. By Chaucer's day the word was quite familiar—

> Throughout every regioun
> Wente this foule trumpet soun,
> As swift as pelet [2] out of gonne,
> When fyr is in the poudre donne.
> > (House of Fame, iii. 551.)

---

[1] *Tom* is also the name of some famous bells, partly chosen, I suppose, for its suggestion of booming resonance.

[2] Both *pellet* and *bullet* were originally used of large projectiles, cannon-balls (cf. F. *boulet*). This sense survives in *bullet-headed*.

But the earliest known *gun* was a catapult or man-gonel. In an inventory of Windsor Castle (1330–1) occurs the item ' una magna balista de cornu quae vocatur *Domina Gunhilda* ', and an allusion to the same stone-hurling engine, by the name of *Gonild*, is found in a political song of still more ancient date. It is probable that the English ' gonners and artellers ' of whom we read in 1344 had as much to do with mangonels as with the new fire-arms. The transition of sense has a parallel in *artillery* (p. 54) and in the British soldier's *bandook*, *bundook*, a rifle, originally an Arabic word for a crossbow.[1]

The name *Gunhilda* is Old Norse and both of its elements mean war, so it is quite possible that, long before the time of our records, this appro-priate name had been conferred by some hardy Norseman on his favourite siege-engine. It will be noticed that in this nomenclature female names are predominant. The shortening to *Gunna*, *Gunn*, is normal, our surname *Gunn* being similarly derived from *Gunhild*, *Gunstan*, *Gunweald*, or some other *Gun-* name.

This early example of a common noun derived from a rather fantastically chosen proper name emboldens me to mention conjectural etymologies which I have put forward elsewhere for two other words from the age of chivalry, viz. our *baldric* and the common Old French *bliaud*, the silken tunic

---

[1] The title of *Bibars Bendocdar*, the Mameluke who became Sultan of Egypt in the 13th century, means something like ' master of the ordnance '.

worn by a knight over his armour. The first, found also in Old French, is identical in form with the Teutonic name *Baldric*, bold-mighty. Though no longer used baptismally, this survives in several surnames, e.g. English *Baldry*, French *Baudry*, etc. As the *baldric* was a very ornate piece of equipment, it seems possible that some medieval knight or yeoman, one with enough imagination to name the *Lady Gunhilda*, may have given this suitable label to part of his equipment. The *bliaud* was also a gay piece of attire. The word corresponds in form to the Teutonic name *Blithwald*, blithe-powerful, the name of the original owner of *Fontainebleau*, earlier *Fontainebliaud*, and, in medieval Latin, *Fontana Blidaldi*. These origins seem to me as plausible as the derivation of French *jaquette*, and of the still earlier *georget*, a kind of doublet. With the latter we may compare *jerkin*, corresponding to the synonymous German dialect *jürken*, apparently a diminutive from *Jürg*, dialect form of *Georg*.

CHAPTER v

MUGS AND JUGS

THE *toby* which solaced Mr. Varden was a 'goodly jug of well-browned clay, fashioned in the form of an old gentleman, atop of whose bald head was a fine white froth answering to his wig' (Barnaby Rudge, ch. iv). Dickens was apparently the first to give the name *toby* [1] to a beer-jug, as also to Punch's dog (Old Curiosity Shop, ch. xviii). In Tom Brown's Schooldays (ch. i) such a vessel is punningly called *Toby Philpot*. The witticism is an old one, for *Toby Philpot* is a devotee of the brown jug in O'Keefe's Poor Soldier (1782). Drinking-vessels are often associated with personal names, partly, no doubt, as a result of their being sometimes shaped to resemble the human form or countenance. This association persists in the vulgar use of *mug*, face, whence the actor's 'mugging up', more politely 'making up', as a preliminary to appearing before the public, a term later borrowed by the candidate who has to appear before the examiner. And here it may be remarked that anyone who believes he knows the English language

---

[1] The *toby* of *high toby* and *low toby*, old cant names for the professions of highwayman and footpad respectively, is unconnected. It is the Shelta (see p. 142, n. 2) word for road.

might well look up a few familiar monosyllables in the Oxford Dictionary. There he will find, for instance, fifteen provisionally distinguished *mugs*, viz. eight nouns and seven verbs. The origin of *mug*, a vessel, is quite unknown. It is of late appearance (16th century) and somewhat similar words are found in Low German, in the Scandinavian languages, and in Norman French. The fact that so many words of this class, including the very comprehensive *pot*, are still a puzzle to etymologists inclines me to conjecture that in some cases they spring from personal names.

Jug, which also appears in the 16th century, has no parallel in other languages. Wedgwood, in his Etymological Dictionary (1857), suggested that it was identical with the female name *Jug*, well attested by the early dictionaries as an old pet-form of *Jane* or *Joan*. Like many such familiar names (see p. 85), *Jug* had a disparaging sense,[1] and was used especially of a soldier's wench. The choice of the name would be just as natural as that of *jack* for an infinite number of objects or of *sukey* (an almost equally violent perversion of *Susan*), used in many rural parts of England for a tea-kettle, which the Australian bushman prefers to call a *billy*. The use of *jug* or *jug-jug* for the note of the nightingale, which to an Eastern ear sounded *bulbul*, may be an attempt to associate the imitative with a familiar name. The name was actually

[1] The Oxford Dictionary has an interesting quotation showing the identity of *Joan* and *Jug* and the contemptuous force of the latter—" Mistris Joan has quite forgot that she was once Jugge " (1631).

used for the bird itself, a fact not recorded by the
Oxford Dictionary—

> *Jug*, a nightingale : *Philomela*.
> (Littleton, Latin Dict., 1673.)

A strong argument for the identity of *jug* with
the female name is the similar use of *jack* or *black
jack* for a leathern drinking-vessel. Shakespeare
couples this with *jill* in a somewhat obscure passage
in which the commentators agree that familiar
names of male and female servants have a secondary
reference to ' mugs and jugs '—

> Where's the cook ? Is supper ready, the house trimmed,
> rushes strewed, cobwebs swept ; the serving-men in their new
> fustian, the white stockings, and every officer his wedding gar-
> ment on ? Be the jacks fair within, the jills fair without, the
> carpets laid and everything in order ?
> (Taming of the Shrew, iv. 1.)

A more modern example is *brown George*,[1] used in
dialect of an earthen pitcher. A very ancient one
is *jub*, a Middle English form of the name *Job*,[2]
which may even have helped to suggest the later
jug—

> With breed and chese and good ale in a jubbe.
> (Chaucer, A. 3628.)

The word is used more than once by Chaucer, and
is spelt *jobbe* in another 14th-century document.

These personal names of vessels beginning with
j- entitle us to conjecture a similar origin for some
later words. *Jorum* (18th century) is most familiar

[1] Also a kind of wig and a coarse loaf. With the latter cf.
the synonymous French *gros-Guillaume* and the contemporary
English *tommy*, ' grub ', for the earlier *Tommy Brown*.

[2] Whence the surnames *Jubb, Jupp*.

to us in the obsolescent *jorum of punch*. Grose
defines it as 'a jug or large pitcher'. *Jeroboam*
is similarly used by Scott, but is now applied to
a bottle of vast capacity. A London wine-mer-
chant has gone one better with a *rehoboam*, equal
to two *jeroboams*. These have been conjecturally
derived from *King Joram*, who ' brought with him
vessels of silver, and vessels of gold, and vessels
of brass' (2 Samuel viii. 10), and *Jeroboam*, son
of Nebat, who ' made Israel to sin ' (1 Kings xiv.
16) ; but this is hardly etymology. In all probability they were arbitrarily chosen, as names with
a pleasantly convivial roll, with a vague reminiscence of the much earlier *jack, jug*, etc., and perhaps
of *jordan*.

The vulgar sense of this word is already in Chaucer,
who also has it in its original meaning of physician's
vessel, probably used in connection with the only
medical diagnosis known to the Middle Ages. The
Oxford Dictionary says ' origin uncertain '. Now
Jordan was a very common medieval font-name
(cf. German *Jordan*, Dutch *Jordaen*, French *Jour-
dain*, Italian *Giordano*, etc.), surviving now as a
surname along with the derivative forms *Judd,
Judson, Judkins, Jukes*. In the Hundred Rolls
(1273) we find Roger fil. Jurdan in Cambridgeshire
and Robert fil. Jordan in Oxfordshire. This unique
adoption of a river-name seems to be due to some
mystical identification of the *Jordan* with *John the
Baptist*. In fact Trevisa, in his 14th-century translation of Higden's Polychronicon, speaks of *Jordan*
or *Johan* (the Baptist). This name may have been

given to a vessel for some reason quite obscure to the modern mind. It has a later parallel in the Shakespearean *jakes*, a latrine, which dates from the early 16th century. Its older spelling was *jaques*,[1] and no doubt it is the familiar French name. The French soldier's name for the convenience is *Jules*.[2] Elizabethan humour sometimes converted *a jakes* into *Ajax* (e.g. Love's Labour Lost, v. 2), hence the title of Harington's work (p. 140).

The Oxford Dictionary accidentally omits the vulgar sense of *jerry*. Hotten's Slang Dictionary (1864) says it is used by Swift. If this is so, Hotten's derivation from *jeroboam* (v.s.) is impossible, as the slang application of the latter word is only recorded from the 19th century. The late 17th century called the object *Oliver's skull* in derision of the great Protector. Like most familiar names *jerry* has a number of slang and dialect senses, current or obsolete, some of which are connected with the *Tom* and *Jerry* of Pierce Egan's Life in London ; or the Day and Night Scenes of Jerry Hawthorn and his elegant Friend, Corinthian Tom (1821 ff.). A *jerry-shop* is both a low beer-house and a shop run by the ' works ', at which, before the Truck Act, employees were compelled to take part of their wages in goods. *Jerry-come-*

[1] The unpleasant associations of *Jakes*, once a common surname, have led to the modern reversion to the spelling *Jaques*.

[2] Also *Colin, Thomas, Eudoxie, Madame Bernard, Madame Durand*. The scatological motif is, like the sexual, one of the most prolific in word-creation, as in ' humour '.

tumble, jerry-go-nimble are dialect words for a circus performer—

> They took me to Greenhill Fair and into a great large jerry-go-nimble show, where there were women-folk riding round—standing upon horses, with hardly anything on but their smocks.
>
> (Hardy, Far from the Madding Crowd, ch. viii.)

Jerry sneak, a mean-spirited character in Foote's Mayor of Garratt (1763), was once as proverbial as John Poole's *Paul Pry* (1825), with his ' I hope I don't intrude '. The most familiar of the *jerry* words is *jerry-built,* in use at Liverpool about 1860, the locality rather favouring the conjecture that it may be a corruption of the nautical *jury-*, as in *jury-mast, jury-rigged,* etc.

A vessel of which the personal name origin is certain is *bellarmine*, originally designed by Protestants of the Netherlands as a caricature of *Cardinal Bellarmine* (+ 1621). Introduced into Scotland it became known as a *greybeard*, which is still in use for a whiskey-jar—

> The greatest sort, they say,
> Are like stone pots, with beards that do reach down
> Unto their knees.
>
> (Cartwright, Lady Errant, 1651.)

Another once familiar word, apparently of a similar type, is *goddard*, a drinking-cup, which the Oxford Dictionary records from the 15th century. This is Old French *godart*, now represented by *godet*, a small bowl. It is identical in form with an old Teutonic personal name, meaning god-powerful, well established in several European countries as a modern surname. This suggests a possible origin

for *goblet*, which is French *gobelet*, a diminutive of
Old French *gobeau* or *gobel*. All three of these
words are familiar French surnames derived from
the same original as *goblin* (pp. 79–81). To the question why this name should have been chosen for
a drinking-vessel one can only reply ' Why *toby* ?
Why *goddard* ? Why *jorum* ? ' One might, however, conjecture some sort of punning association
with *gober*, to swallow.

A *demijohn* is a huge bottle cased in wicker for
safety in transport and generally furnished with
handles. It is an 18th-century corruption of French
dame-jeanne, which dates from the 17th century.
The English form was further contorted in slang
into *jemmy-john*. The corresponding Italian and
Spanish names are *damigiana* and *damajuana*. The
word has been much discussed and attempts have
been made to connect it with a supposed Latin
dimidiana, from *dimidium*, half. But it is comparatively modern and never seems to have meant
a half of any other measure, being, in fact, the
largest of all bottles (as much as fifteen gallons !).
As it is essentially a nautical word—

dame-jane : les matelots appellent ainsi une grosse bouteille de
verre couverte de natte.

(Th. Corneille, 1694),

there can be little doubt that this portly vessel
was thus nicknamed by sailors, though it is uncertain to which language it originally belonged.
This view is supported by the fact that a very
large *demijohn* is also called in French a *jacqueline*.

Tankard seems to have originated in England,

being more than two centuries older than the archaic
Dutch and French forms. It originally meant, from
c. 1300, a tub-like vessel bound with hoops for
carrying liquids or solids. Wyclif uses it (Zechariah
v. 6) to render the *amphora* of the Vulgate, where
the Authorized Version has reverted to the Hebrew
ephah, a measure of several bushels. From the
15th century it is recorded as the name of a hooped
wooden drinking-vessel. As there is no clue to its
origin, I suggest that it is identical with the surname *Tankard*, found in England since the time
of Edward I. This is from an old Teutonic personal name related to *Tancred*. One of its bearers
must have founded *Tancarville* (Seine–Inf.), whence
our surname *Tankerville*. It is even possible that
the fame of the crusader *Tancred* [1] may have had
something to do with the choice of the name, even
as our remote ancestors gave to an excellent apple
the name *Cœur-de-lion*, now reduced to *codlin*. [2]
There may even have been a vague metathetic
association with Greco-Latin *cantharus*, which, like
its Romance derivatives, is glossed *tankard* in the
earliest dictionaries.

Here is one more conjecture. *Puncheon*, a large
cask, comes from the French *poinçon* (13th century),
whence also Italian *punzone*. In all three languages
the word also means a piercing instrument (in
English shortened to *punch*), derived from Latin
pungere, but no connection can be established be-

---

[1] The names are not identical, but near enough. Cf. Shakespeare's identification of *Tybalt* with *Tibert* (p. 133).

[2] See my Words Ancient and Modern, p. 23.

tween the two senses. I believe that the cask
takes its name from *Pontius Pilate*, to whom we
owe a large number of French and English surnames. Of course no child was ever christened
Pontius, but, as a nickname, probably conferred
on those who had played the rôle of the Roman
governor in the Passion Play, it is quite common.
The Bottin contains some thirty surnames [1] which
can be derived from *Pontius*, e.g. *Pons, Ponce,* [2]
Ponson, Poinson, Poinsot, etc. Many of these have
passed into England—*Poyntz, Punch, Punshon,* and
the thinned [3] forms *Pinch, Pinchin.* In the light
of the examples quoted in this chapter, it does
not seem outside the bounds of possibility that
this formidable name may have been given to a
formidable barrel. It is more imaginative than
Old Tom—

Old Tom : 'tis a cask or barrel containing strong gin, and
thence, by a natural transition, the liquor itself.

(Slang Dict., 1823),

and as reasonable as *hogshead*, which dates from
the 14th century and has been adopted by most
of the Teutonic languages, with the substitution of
ox- for *hogs-* (Low German *oxhoft*, Danish *oxehoved*,
etc.).

Before leaving *Pontius Pilate*, we may note that

[1] On the extraordinary multiplication of French surnames
from one original personal name see my Surnames, p. 282.

[2] This is the regular form of the name. The saying ' envoyer
quelqu'un de Ponce à Pilate ' (Italian has, more correctly,
' mandare da Erode a Pilato '), i.e. from pillar to post, seems to
be due to a confused recollection of Luke xxiii (so also in German).

[3] Cf. *Jim* from James, *Binks* from Banks, and Mr. Manta-
lini's *demnition*.

pawnbrokers were thus nicknamed in the 18th century (Grose), and that the title *Pontius Pilate's Bodyguard* has been borne by the Royal Scots ' from time immemorial '. Traditionally this is due to the boast of one of their officers that, if they had been on guard at the Sepulchre, they would not have slept at their posts !

There is no doubt as to the nicknaming of medieval citizens from characters in the Passion Play. In the 13th century we find such names as Seman Herodes and Alan Pilate. It is to the representation of *Herod* as a ranting tyrant that we owe Shakespeare's to *out-Herod Herod* (Hamlet, iii. 2), on which so many variations have been played, e.g. Oscar Wilde aspired sarcastically to *out-Kipling Henley*. In my Surnames (p. 207) I have noted the fees paid in 1490 to the Coventry smiths who played the various rôles. Pilate (4*d.*) seems to have been much less important than Caiaphas and Herod (3*s.* 4*d.* each), but Pilate's wife received 2*s.* The Devil and Judas were equal with 1*s.* 6*d.*, while Peter and Malchus got 1*s.* 4*d.* each. *Malchus* seems to have made, no doubt owing to the sword incident, a special appeal to the audience, though his name is only once mentioned in the Bible.[1] Migliorini (see p. 1, n. 1) gives (pp. 121–3), from various Romance languages, a large number of witticisms connected with this unimportant name, e.g. at Liège it is used of an animal with one ear,

---

[1] ' Then Simon Peter having a sword drew it, and smote the high priest's servant, and cut off his right ear. The servant's name was Malchus ' (John xviii. 10).

and at Verona of a ' heavy-handed ' individual,
which is almost as confused as Mrs. Gamp's allusion
to *Jonadge's belly*.[1] Scarron, first husband of
Madame de Maintenon, has *malchus*, a sword, in
his Virgile Travesti, and in the 17th century the
name was applied in French to a high-backed arm-
chair with only one ' ear ' against which to rest
the head. *Malchus* is also the hero of one of the
best genuine howlers I have come across. A schoolboy, asked to explain certain Scriptural phrases,
thus elucidated ' First the blade, then the ear '
(Mark iv. 28)—' These words were said by Saint
Peter, as he silently approached the high priest's
servant.'

[1] So also, the shellfish that we call *ormer* or *sea-ear* (French
oreille de mer) is in Istria *recia de Malco*, but in Languedoc
aurelho de san Peire.

CHAPTER VI

MUMBO-JUMBO

IT is said that our dialects are provided with some forty names for the Enemy of Mankind, otherwise known as the Evil One, the Prince of Darkness, His Satanic Majesty, etc., circumlocutions, sometimes half-propitiatory, which aim at avoiding a dreaded name. One of his most picturesque titles is the *Earl of Hell*, and it is refreshing to find that ' as black as the Earl of Hell's waistcoat ', as a description of a dark night, is still used by the imaginative. Burns's Address to the Deil begins—

> O thou ! whatever title suit thee,
> *Auld Hornie, Satan, Nick* or *Clootie*.[1]

Edgar, in his character of a *Tom o' Bedlam*, proclaims that—

> The prince of darkness is a gentleman,
> *Modo*, he's called, and *Mahu*.
>
> (Lear, iii. 4.)

These names are taken, along with ' the foul fiend *Flibberdegibbet* ' (ibid.), from Archbishop Harsnett's Declaration of Egregious Popish Impostures (1603), in which *Flibberdegibbet*, *Frateretto*, *Hoberdidance* and *Tocobatto* are enumerated as the four devils of

[1] From Scottish *cloot*, hoof.

the morris-dance.[1] The earlier meaning of *flibber-degibbet*, and one which survives colloquially, was a prattling, flighty woman. It is lengthened (? by association with *gibbet*) from a still older *flibbergib*,[2] used in a sermon by Bishop Latimer. Some of Dante's invented demons have more obvious names, e.g. *Graffiacan* (Inferno, xxii. 34), from *graffiare*, to claw, *Cagnazzo* (ibid., xxii. 106), which means dog-like.

As we have frequently had occasion to remark, all names were originally significant, gradually becoming mere labels as they acquired the capital initial. Greek *diabolos*, which penetrated with the missionaries into every European language, means slanderer. The fact that *demon*, from Greek *daimōn*, tutelary genius, and *imp*, offshoot, ' scion ', have both assumed a Satanic sense seems to point to the general triumph of evil over good. Anglo-Saxon also rendered the foreign word by *feond*,[3] enemy, surviving in the poetic *foul fiend*. This persisted, by the side of *devil*, in Middle English, as in Chaucer's version of the old proverb that ' He that sups with the devil must have a long spoon '—

> Therfore bihoveth hire a ful long spoon
> That shal ete with a feend.

(F. 602),

---

[1] Moorish dance ; cf. French *danse moresque*. Known in England from the 15th century. In spite of the name, the characters usually belonged to the Robin Hood saga.

[2] The Oxford Dictionary suggests no etymology. There is a very widely used dialect *jib*, mouth, lower lip, used in Essex especially in the sense of talk, ' jaw ', so that the word may contain the idea of ' chin-wagging '.

[3] The present participle of *feogan*, to hate.

and occurs regularly in Bible translations as late as Tyndale.

The proper Biblical name for the devil is *Satan*, Hebrew for adversary. *Belial*, worthlessness, is, in the Old Testament, a personification of evil. The New Testament identified him with Satan, and Milton made him one of the fallen angels. The name is especially familiar in his ' sons of Belial '. *Beelzebub*, lord of flies, i.e. monarch of one of the great plagues of the East, was originally the god of Ekron. The first part of his name is identical with *Baal*, lord, the deity of the Phoenicians, and with the final syllable of *Hannibal*. *Lucifer*, the morning star, ' light-bearer ',[1] is identified with Satan by a mystical interpretation of Isaiah xiv. 10— ' How art thou fallen from heaven, O Lucifer, son of the morning ! ' The early Fathers adopted *Lucifer* for Satan before his ' fall ', which was regarded as due to his ' pride '. In the early 19th century his name was applied to a match, which the inventor had originally called *promethean* [2] (see p. 6). *Apollyon*, Greek for destroyer, is used in Revelation ix. 11 to interpret the Hebrew *Abaddon*, destruction. Bunyan made the name familiar.

Mankind, not satisfied with all these designations of his Enemy, has added *Demogorgon* and *Mephistopheles*, special fiends who are sometimes identified with their principal. The former, a deity invoked

---

[1] Cf. the synonymous Greek *phosphorus*.

[2] A more ' volcanic ' type, long disused by all good smokers, was a *vesuvian*. Cf. *etna*, a 19th-century device for rapid boiling.

in magic rites, was made literary by Boccaccio. The name is apparently due to a wrong reading, in a scholiast of the 5th century, for Greek *dēmiourgon* (acc.), demiurge, the world-creator in the Platonic philosophy. The more familiar *Mephistopheles* is comparatively modern, first occurring, as *Mephostophiles*, in the German Faustbuch of 1587. He was almost at once introduced into England by Marlowe and was known to Ancient Pistol (Merry Wives, i. 1). In English he is a type of the sardonic. The origin of the name is quite unknown. It may have been intended to denote a lover of ' mephitic ' vapours.[1]

Mephistopheles belongs rather to the long list of popular creations which were fantastically used in place of the Biblical names of the devil. The almost friendly and familiar ring of some of these may perhaps be traced to that underground paganism which has always persisted even among Christianized races, and which, even now, is by no means extinct. As the old Scotchwoman explained, when rebuked for praying for the Deil, ' It's as well to have friends everywhere.' The earliest periphrasis in English is Anglo-Saxon *se ealda*, the old 'un, and this adjective is very persistent in his modern petnames. Defoe calls him the *old gentleman*. On *Old Nick*, recorded for the 17th century, though probably in much earlier use, a great deal of nonsense has been written. One theory derived him

[1] Cf. *Syphilis*, sive Morbus Gallicus, a poem (1530) by Fracastoro, a physician of Verona, in which *Syphilis* is a shepherd. The name may be the Ovidian shepherd-name *Siphylus* contorted so as to suggest ' swine-lover '.

from the obsolete *nicker*, water-sprite, 'kelpie', Anglo-Saxon *nicor*.[1] This puts him rather 'out of his element'. Samuel Butler, in Hudibras, humorously identified him with *Niccolò Machiavelli*, as 'Ingoldsby' did *jingo* [2] with *Saint Gengulfus*, and I have seen this seriously repeated in a recent book, which also traces *news* to the four cardinal points of the compass (*N.E.W.S.*)! The theologically minded used to point to the early heretical deacon *Nicholas*—

> Thou hatest the deeds of the Nicolaitanes, which I also hate.
>
> (Revelation ii. 6),

and others to *Saint Nicholas*, whose reputation was rather variegated, for he was, among other things, the patron saint of highwaymen, 'clerks of Saint Nicholas' (1 Henry IV, ii. 1). In all probability the name was taken at random to express a kind of affectionate intimacy, just as, at an earlier date, we find *dickens* (Merry Wives, iii. 2), a familiar form of *Richard*, and later *Old Harry*, more respectfully used in 'By the *Lord Harry*!' (Congreve). The more dignified German *Urian*, used both of the Devil and of Thingummy or What's-his-name, is equally inexplicable.

Old Scratch, which Grose connects with 'claws',

---

[1] Cf. German *nixe*, whence our *nix*, *nixie*, introduced, along with *werwolf*, *erlking*, etc., when we discovered German literature, c. 1800. See my More Words Ancient and Modern.

[2] Probably from the Basque word for God. The characteristic sense dates from the famous music-hall song (1878)—'We don't want to fight, but by jingo, if we do.'

does not belong to this group. It is for earlier *scrat*, from Old Norse *skratte*, goblin. It may be noted that German has *nickel* (for *Nicolaus*), a goblin, whence the name of a metal originally regarded by copper-miners as useless and deceptive.[1]

For to *play the dickens* the Kentish farmer says, or did, when I was a boy, to *play old Pout*, which I take to be a corrupted survival of Middle English *Pouk*, frequently used by Langland for the Devil, but, since Shakespeare's *Puck*, a tricksy sprite identified with *Robin Goodfellow* and *Hobgoblin* (see p. 81). *Puck* had a diminutive *puckle*, surviving as a surname of nickname origin. Reginald Scot, in his Discoverie of Witchcraft (1584), tells of ' the puckle, Tom thombe,[2] hob goblin and such other bugs '. *Puck* is also, in some of our dialects, applied to the nightjar or goatsucker, which has an uncanny reputation.

The probability that *Nick* and *Harry*, as applied to the Devil, are merely popular names taken at random is confirmed by the wide nomenclature associated with the minor fiend called by scientists *ignis fatuus*.[3] The most general name, and one that is common in figurative use, is *will o' the wisp*, where *wisp* means torch, but *jack o' lantern*, originally a contemptuous name for a night watchman, is almost equally familiar. In dialect we find also *Billy wi' t' wisp, Hob lantern, Kitty candlestick,*

[1] In full *kupfernickel*, adapted from Swedish ; cf. *cobalt* (p. 79, n. 3).
[2] The ' Barnum ' use of *Tom Thumb*, originally a diminutive goblin, dates only from the 19th century.
[3] This is a medieval Latin translation of French *feu follet*.

F

Peggy lantern, *Dick a Tuesday*, *Gillian burnt-tail*, etc. Milton calls it *friar's lantern*—

> She was pinched and pulled, she said,
> And he by friar's lantern led
>
> (Allegro, 103),

which perhaps accounts for Scott's erroneous use of *Friar Rush*, the hero of a German legend which has nothing to do with the *ignis fatuus*—

> Better we had through mire and bush
> Been lantern-led by Friar Rush.
>
> (Marmion, iv. 1.)

In the neighbourhood of Béthune the *will o' the wisp* is called *arlequin*, which brings us to a very interesting word.

Harlequin, as we know him, is one of the group of pantomime characters who belonged originally to the Italian *commedia dell' arte*. But, before becoming the associate of *Columbine* and *Pantaloon*,[1] he was a medieval fiend, some of whose diabolical features persist in details of his costume and in his supposed invisibility to the other actors. His name is found, from the 12th century onward, in Old French, with a large number of variants (*Herlechin*, *Hierlekin*, *Hellequin*, *Hernequin*, *Herlewin*, etc.). He is represented as the demon leader of a demon band of

---

[1] *Columbine* is from Latin *columba*, a dove. *Pantaloon* was originally a Venetian dotard, *Pantaleone* being a favourite name at Venice. For the application of his name to a garment cf. *knickerbockers*, from the original illustrations to *Diedrich Knickerbocker's* (i.e. Washington Irving's) History of Old New York. Another character of the *commedia* was *Scaramouch*, a cowardly braggart dressed in black, intended as a caricature of the Spanish Don. The name comes from Italian *scaramuccia*, skirmish.

hunters, galloping across country at night or heard passing through the air. The myth is an old one, and it is probable that it came to Normandy, where the superstition still persists, with the Norsemen, to be later vulgarized and Christianized into a legend of the unquiet spirits of the damned.

In the Middle Ages *Harlequin* degenerated into a comic devil of street performances, eventually annexed by the Italian *commedia*, and, as the old rustic superstition did not die out, the original fiend divided, as it were, into two personalities.

As is usual in such legends, *Harlequin* became identified with various more or less historical characters, e.g. with *Herod*, with a rather vague *Hernequin*, Count of Boulogne, and, by a wild anachronism, with *Charles Quint*, i.e. Charles V. of France, who died in 1380, and who, in this version of the legend, is confused with Charles Martel, victor over the Moors in 732. But these are all edifying ' explanations ', tending to show the punishment of the wicked.

The earliest account (v. i.) describes the *familia Herlechini*, rendered in Old French by *la mesnie*[1] *Hellequin* and in Middle English (Langland) by *Hurlewayne's meyne* or *kynne*. Later he becomes in English *Hellwain*, mentioned by Harsnett (see p. 68), and his last incarnation in this country is as *Herne the Hunter*, who haunted Windsor Forest with his demon band. He is mentioned repeatedly in the Merry Wives of Windsor.

[1] Old French for household, retinue, whence the Shakespearean *meiny* (Lear, ii. 4) and the derivative *menial*.

Hardly any word has excited more etymological curiosity. The literature on the subject is immense,[1] and conjectural derivations are numerous and fantastic. The earliest records of the demon's appearance are delightfully naive. Ordericus Vitalis, writing in Latin c. 1130, tells how the wild hunt was encountered on January 1, 1091, by a priest named Gauchelin, who was even able to identify some of the riders ! The *familia* was led by *Herlechinus*, of gigantic stature and armed with a huge club. The ladies of the band, who rode on side-saddles studded with white-hot nails, were occasionally lifted a cubit by the wind and then dropped back in such a way that ' in natibus vulnerabantur '. Walter Map, in his De Nugis Curialium (c. 1200), informs us that the *Herlething*, the demon retinue of a British King *Herla*, was last seen in Herefordshire in the first year of Henry II., several Welshmen having observed its final plunge into the Wye ! Allusions to the *mesnie Hellequin* are common in Old French literature, the strongest association always having been with Normandy. The chap-books of the 17th and 18th centuries perpetuated the legend, and it was from some such source that Scott drew his information (Minstrelsy of the Scottish Border).

Apart from the forced association of *Harlequin* with various historic names, a few other fantastic guesses may be mentioned. He has been derived

---

[1] See especially Driesen, Der Ursprung des Harlekin (Berlin, 1904), and Rühlemann, Etymologie des Wortes *harlequin* (Halle a.S., 1912).

from the town of *Arles*, from the Flemish *hellekint*, child of hell, from Italian *arlotto* and *lecchino*, both meaning glutton, and has been identified with the *Erlking*.[1] The modern Norman name is *hèle-chien*, a product of folk-etymology. The established facts are that the legend belongs to Normandy, that the persistent initial *h-* points to Teutonic origin and the suffix *-kin* to a Flemish diminutive. Rühlemann puts forward confidently as origin the Flemish *hellekin*, little hell. My own conviction, based on much less knowledge, is that it is some familiar personal name, used like the many appellations of the *ignis fatuus*. It is frequently found as *Hennequin* (now a common French surname), from Flemish *Henekin*,[2] i.e. Johnny, but also used as a term of vituperation. The oldest recorded form is *Herlechin*, but who can say how many variants were in existence before the days of Ordericus Vitalis ?

Finally, some forms of the word, and the ' big club ' of the earliest account, rather suggest some intrusion of *Hercules*, who, for the medieval stage, was a ranting tyrant. Hear Bully Bottom—

' My chief humour is for a tyrant ! I could play Ercles rarely, or a part to tear a cat in, to make all split. . . . This is Ercles' vein, a tyrant's vein.'

(Midsummer Night's Dream, i. 2.)

Mr. Allardyce Nicoll, in Masks, Mimes and Miracles, quotes a 16th-century Latinist's description of a man costumed ' ut luderet personam Herculis vel

[1] For the curious history of this word see my More Words Ancient and Modern, p. 184.

[2] Hence our surname *Hankin*.

Harlequini in comedia'; but the late date of the example and the ambiguous force of *vel* make this evidence worthless as far as the original demon rider is concerned : nor does one remember that *Hercules* was much of an equestrian.

The mention of *Hercules* as a stage braggart suggests a word or two on the mysterious *termagant*, which was not applied to a furious virago before the 17th century. In Old French epic *Tervagan* is coupled with *Mahomet* as a ' god ' of the Saracens, the others being *Jupiter*, *Apollo*, and *Nero*, a curious mixture. Of the origin of *Tervagan*, which became in Italian *Trivigante* (Ariosto) and in English *Tervagant*, *Termagaunt*, etc., nothing is known and even the guesses are uninteresting ; but, via the medieval sense of stage bully, the name became a common word for a swashbuckler. Shakespeare uses it in the original sense (Hamlet, iii. 2) and makes Falstaff call Douglas a *termagant Scot* (1 Henry IV., v. 4). The stage-tyrants *Pontius* and *Herod* have already been mentioned (pp. 65–6). *Hector*, who does not appear in that rôle till much later, has had the unusual fate of becoming a verb, meaning to swagger and bully.

Returning to the goblins, we have noticed that one name for the *will o' the wisp* is *hob lantern*. *Hob* is, like *Bob*, a rimed diminutive of *Robert*,[1] and we find it familiarly prefixed to words meaning demons in *hobthrush* and *hobgoblin*. Cotgrave, after giving a full definition of *loup-garou*, a werwolf, adds,

[1] Robert Bruce is called *King Hob* in a satirical poem of the period.

' Also, a hobgoblin, hobthrush, robin-goodfellow '.
And here we may remark that all goblins, including
fairies, were originally unfriendly and unsightly, and
that *Robin Goodfellow* was just as likely to ' pinch the
maidens black and blue ' as to help them in the
dairy ; hence his propitiatory name.   The modern
sense of *fairy* dates approximately from Spenser and
Shakespeare.   A 16th-century lexicographer equates
the word with *hag* and *nightmare*.   The *thrush* of
hobthrush is a perversion of *thurse*,[1] once a common
name for a goblin, and *Hob* just gives the personal
touch, like *Old Nick*.   By regular association with
goblin the name *hob* itself came to mean fairy, imp,
etc.—

> From elves, hobs and fairies,
> That trouble our dairies, . . .
> Defend us, good Heaven.
>
> (Fletcher, c. 1625.)

It would be tempting to linger over *imps*, *trolls*,
bogles, *boggarts*, *bugbears*,[2] etc., but these are not
proper names, while I propose to show that *goblin*
is one.

It seems impossible not to associate the Old
French *gobelin*, evidently a diminutive, with the
synonymous German *kobold*,[3] a tricksy imp.   This

---

[1] A giant of earlier Teutonic mythology, Anglo-Saxon *thyrs* ;
later a wizard, goblin.

[2] An arbitrary elaboration of *bug*, a spectre, probably (like
bogey, *bogle*, *boggart*) of Celtic origin.   The following quotation
from Coverdale's Bible Translation (1535) reads oddly—' Thou
shalt not nede to be afrayed for eny bugges by night ' (Psalm
xci. 5).

[3] The metal *cobalt* was named from this goblin in the same way
as *nickel* (p. 73).

exists as a modern German surname with many
variants (*Goppelt, Kobbold, Koppelt, Kobelt*, etc.),
and this surname must come from the Old High
German personal name *Godbold*, i.e. god-bold.[1]
The corresponding Anglo-Saxon name was *Godbeald*,
whence our surnames *Godbolt* and *Cobbold*. Another
German word for goblin is *oppolt*, corresponding to
the Old High German name *Otbold* (cf. the surnames
Oppold, Oppelt, etc.), in which *Ot-* is cognate with
Anglo-Saxon *Ead-*, wealth, prosperity (as in the
very common *Eadbeald*). With these names we
may compare German *gütchen*, goblin (Goethe's
Faust, ii. 5848), and Middle High German *gütel*, both
diminutives of *god*, or rather of one of the *God*-
names. More familiar is *heinzelmännchen*, a moun-
tain-gnome or wood-spirit, called by Luther simply
Heinzlein. *Hänselmann* is also used in the same
sense, and it need not be said that *Heinz* is the pet
form of *Heinrich*, and that *Hänsel*, i.e. Johnny, is
the brother of *Gretel*, i.e. Peggy.

The name *Godbold* passed, with a great number of
other Teutonic dithematic names,[2] into Old French
as *Gobaud* and is the origin of the surnames *Gobeau,
Gobel, Gobelet* (see p. 63), *Gobelin*, etc. The *Gobelin*
family were famous Parisian dyers and tapestry
workers as early as the 15th century. Louis XIV.
converted their business into a state industry. I
cannot say why both German and French should
have selected this name for an imp. But neither

[1] In such names the word *god* has not a monotheistic sense.
[2] On the popularity of these Teutonic names in France and
their survival as modern surnames see my Surnames, p. 284.

I, nor anyone else, can say why Satan should be associated with *Henry* and *Nicholas*, why the *ignis fatuus* should be called by half a dozen arbitrarily chosen names or why a goblin should be labelled with the baptismal *Hob*. The fact remains that the earliest record of *goblin* is a story by Ordericus Vitalis (see p. 76) of a demon named *Gobelinus* who haunted the neighbourhood of Évreux, and that his name is, like *kobold*, easily derived from a familiar personal name. Myths may go back to pre-history, but, as has been sufficiently shown in this chapter, the names associated with them are commonly given by the people.

When the personal name has definitely become a common noun, the tendency to individualize shows itself in the prefixing of a new personal name, as in *Poll parrot* and *Madge howlet* (p. 124). So, early in the 16th century, we find *Hob goblin*, who is identified with *Puck* (p. 73) and more ingratiatingly addressed as *Robin Goodfellow*—

> Or else you are that shrewd and knavish sprite
> Call'd Robin Goodfellow ; are you not he
> That fright the maidens of the villagery,
> Skim milk, and sometimes labour in the quern,
> And bootless make the breathless housewife churn,
> And sometimes make the drink to bear no barm,
> Mislead night-wanderers, laughing at their harm ?
> Those that Hobgoblin call you and sweet Puck,
> You do their work, and they shall have good luck.
> (Midsummer Night's Dream, ii. 1.)

CHAPTER VII

JACK AND JILL

ONE of the puzzles of name-lore is the process by which the French name *Jacques* (Latin *Jacobus*, from Hebrew) was early confused with *Jankin* or *Jenkin*, and thus came to be regarded as a pet-form of *John*. Since the 15th century *Jack* and *Jill* have been used for lad and lass, replacing the earlier *Jenkin* and *Gillian*. For a time the two pairs of names were used indifferently, the earlier nomenclature still surviving in the 16th century. Tusser tells us that on wake-day, i.e. the eve of the dedication festival of the parish church—

> Every wanton may dance at her will,
> Both Tomkin with Tomlin [1] and Jenkin with Gill.

Still earlier we find *Jenkin* and *Malkin* (see p. 86). The Oxford Dictionary quotes, from a Lutel Sermon (c. 1275), ' Theos prude yungemen that luvieth Malekin, and theos prude maidens that luvieth Janekin.'

Place aux dames ! *Gillian* is the popular form of *Juliana*, which, for some unknown reason, was a favourite medieval font-name. Like most female names in common use it acquired a derogatory sense and became equivalent to wench, light o' love, etc. *Gillian-flirt* and *Gill-flirt* were common terms of

[1] A female name *Tomaline* ; cf. *Thomasine*.

reproach from the 16th century onward, *flirt* having at that period a much stronger sense than now. Cotgrave gives, along with a number of unquotable epithets, *gill* and *flirt* as explanations of the female name *Gaultière*, while the masculine form *Gaultier* [1] (Walter) is defined as ' a mad whorson, mad wag, rakehell, good fellow ; also, a noddy, ninny, gosecap, coxcombe, ideot '. The word *jilt* itself is a contraction of the diminutive *Gillet*, so that *Juliet* and *jilt* are etymological doublets. The usual Old French equivalent for *Jack* and *Jill* is *Robin* et *Marion* (see p. 21), the title of the earliest French ' operetta ' (13th century). The Romans said, though in a more dignified sense, *Gaius* and *Gaia*, for husband and wife, master and mistress.

Female names are curiously subject to fashion and are apt to ' date ' their bearers. Just now nearly all babies of the more important sex are being christened *Jane* or *Ann*, which were decidedly out of fashion a few generations ago. A decade or two earlier *Joan* had a great vogue, a name which, in Shakespeare's time, was equivalent to a kitchen-wench. Thus the Bastard Faulconbridge, on being knighted by the king, remarks, ' Well, now can I make any Joan a lady ' (King John, i. 1) ; and, in Love's Labour's Lost, v. 2, she appears in still less attractive guise—

> To-whit, to-who, a merry note,
> While greasy Joan doth keel the pot.

---

[1] *Bon Gaultier* is perhaps still in French use for a boon companion, and one remembers the *Bon Gaultier Ballads* in which Aytoun and Theodore Martin collaborated.

The saying that ' *Jack* is as good as his master ' has as an early parallel ' *Joan* is as good as my lady '. My own ' reaction ' to the name *Susan* is a vision of a sturdy young woman garbed in ' print ' and armed with a mop or other domestic implement, a picture compounded of a succession of domestic *Susans* passing before the eyes of early childhood. Similar was the reaction of the poet Gray—

> No dolphin came, no nereid stirred ;
> No cruel Tom nor Susan heard !
> A favourite has no friends :
>> (Ode on the death of a favourite cat drowned
>> in a tub of goldfishes.)

It is symptomatic of the game of general post now being played by the classes and masses that *Susan* is taking refuge, with *Betty*, *Peggy*, *Jane* and *Ann*, among the aristocracy, while *Gladys* and *Muriel* reign below stairs, the former name being given also, I understand, to the effigy of a tea-shop waitress which is the mascot of the Royal Dental Hospital. A modern Quarles would be inclined to reverse the names in the line—' Courtly Mildred dies, while country Madge survives.'

A great number of familiar feminine names are applied to various beasts and birds (Chapter IX), and also to domestic implements and gadgets of various kinds (Chapter IV), e.g. the Oxford Dictionary gives half a dozen figurative uses of the name *Kitty* or of words which have been popularly assimilated to that name. The most widely used name of this type is *doll*, pet-form of *Dorothy*, with which one may compare the synonymous French *marionnette*.

All of which goes to show that man in his simplest
form, uncorrupted by education, tends to create his
vocabulary in the same way as the infant.

Then we have a group of names used in a contemptuous or more than contemptuous sense. In
Walloon a girl is a *Trine* (*Catherine*), as also in
German (especially in *dumme Trine*), while in
America she is a *Jane* and in many parts of France
a *Marie*, often with an addition, e.g. *Marie bon-bec*,
a chatterbox. *Marie-salope*, the second element of
which means slut, is applied also to a harbour-
dredger, and, in the ' argot des poilus ', to a field
kitchen ! *Mag* or *Meg* has been used since the 16th
century of a hoyden or boisterous woman, especially
with reference to *Long Meg of Westminster*, a notorious virago whose Life and Pranks (1582) ran
through many editions. To her we possibly owe
also *Mag's diversions*, though there is no early record.
Dickens's first idea for the title of David Copperfield
was ' Mag's Diversions, being the personal history
of Mr. Thomas Mag, the younger, of Blunderstone
House'. Much older is the obsolete *Mag's tales*
(14th century) for old wives' tales.

Lower in the moral scale comes *Moll*, a name
borne in the 16th century by the notorious *Moll
Cutpurse*, a real character whose exploits were
utilized by Middleton and Dekker in their Roaring
Girl (1611). This name seems definitely ostracized,
but the diminutive *Molly*, once in almost equally
bad odour, has now returned to favour. *Molly-
coddle*, for the 18th-century *Miss Molly*, an effem-
inate fellow, perhaps contains a punning allusion

to Latin *mollis*, soft, as elementary word-plays are often to be found lurking in the background of this region of vocabulary, e.g. *Katy* and *Kitty*, recorded in the same objectionable senses as *Moll*, have been helped in their descent by association with *cat* and *kitten*, and the Scottish *katy-handed*, left-handed, is an obvious adaptation of the synonymous Danish *keithaandet*. With the derogatory sense of some of these names we may compare French *Catin* (*Catherine*) and *Goton* (*Margot*), with their very offensive implication.

Two female names are of special philological interest. *Malkin* is explained by the Promptorium Parvulorum (1440) as a pet-form of *Matilda*, but has, I think, more to do with *Mary*. In fact, it is found applied to the *Maid Marian* of the Robin Hood pageant. *Mal* is the oldest pet-form of *Mary*. It was the name of the poor widow's sheep in the Nun's Priest's Tale—

> Thre large sowes hadde she and namo ;
> Three keen and eek a sheep that highte Malle.
> (Chaucer, B. 4020.)

From the 13th century *Malkin* was used as a general disparaging term for a woman or girl, especially an untidy woman, drab, slut, slattern, a maid-servant—

> Ran Colle,[1] oure dogge, and Talbot, and Gerland,
> And Malkyn, with a dystaf in her hand
> (Chaucer, B. 4574),

a mop or oven-broom, a scarecrow, a rag-doll, a cat, and, in the north, as a name for the hare. Many of these uses survive in dialect, and Tennyson

[1] Pet-form of *Nicholas*. Hence *collie* (dog).

writes, in The Princess (v. 25), of ' a draggled maw-kin, that tends her bristled grunters in the sludge '. Earlier than any of these names is the solitary occurrence (c. 1200) of *malkin*, a female spectre. The earliest record of *grimalkin*, a cat, is Shake-speare's *Gray Malkin* (Macbeth, i. 1), addressed by the witches to the fiend, presumably appearing in tabby form. With *Malkin* goes *Mabel* (i.e. *Amabel*, the lovable), applied, in the Middle English form *Mably*, to a witch (Chaucer, D. 1626), to the grisly *Queen Mab*, who was transformed in Tudor times into an attractive sprite, to an oven-broom (*mapple* = *malkin* in the Promptorium Parvulorum), later reduced to *map*, *mop*, and to a disorderly dress, as in the *mobled queen* of Hamlet (ii. 2), whence our *mob-cap*. As the hare is called *malkin*, so the rabbit is called in Scottish *mapkin*.

To enumerate all the transferred and colloquial senses of *Jack* would require a fair-sized book. As applied to people it is usually contemptuous or hostile, *Jack* being essentially the representative of the ' lower orders '—

> Since every Jack became a gentleman,
> There's many a gentle person made a Jack.
> (Richard III., i. 3).

Hence *jack in office*, *every man jack*, *cheapjack*, etc. Even *Jack tar*, now admirative, was no doubt originally used by those who thought, with Dr. Johnson, that no man ever went to sea who had wit enough to get himself inside a gaol. Much earlier is *Jack sailor*. *Jack* is also applied, like other familiar names, to all sorts of gadgets and mechanical

devices, especially those which replace servile agency.
No doubt *bootjack* (p. 51) originally meant a varlet,
for, though dictionaries do not record it, we find
jackboots applied to a hotel servant c. 1820.
The archaic *jack*, leather jerkin, coat of mail, with
its diminutive *jacket*, forms of which are found in
various European languages, is also no doubt from
the name *Jacques*, though its ultimate connection
with *Jacques Bonhomme* (p. 158) is a matter of conjecture. The *jackboot* was perhaps so called from a
vague resemblance to the leathern drinking-vessel
called a *jack* or *black jack*.

But the most interesting part of *Jack's* activities
is that which illustrates the popular fancy for
personifying certain human types by the addition of
a Christian name. A curious modern example is
the Australian *jackaroo*, green hand, new chum,
obviously modelled on *kangaroo*. *Jack fool* once
ran parallel with *Tomfool*—

> ' Go fro the wyndow, Jakke-fool,' she said.
> (Chaucer, A. 3708.)

Jack Drum's entertainment, the chucking out of an
unwelcome guest, is *Tom Drum's* in Holinshed and
John Drum's in Shakespeare (All's Well, iii. 6).
Then we have a force of nature personified in *Jack
Frost*, impudence in the archaic *Jack sauce*—

> See you now, his reputation is as arrant a villain, and a Jack
> sauce, as ever his plack shoe trod upon Got's ground and his
> earth.
>
> (Henry V., iv. 7),

and those two mysterious individuals *Jack Adams*
and *Jack Robinson*. The former equivalent of a

fool was in navy use till quite recently, while Miss
Burney is our earliest recorded authority for *Jack
Robinson* as a measure of rapid articulation. *Jack
a' Lent* was the Shakespearean *Aunt Sally*, and the
following quotation suggests a curiously modern
picture—

> Thou . . . travelledst to Hampstead Heath on Ash Wednes-
> day, where thou didst stand six weeks the Jack a' Lent, for
> boys to hurl, three throws a penny, at thee.
>
> (Ben Jonson, Tale of a Tub, iv. 3.)

Jack Sprat, of the nursery rime, originally meant
(16th century) a dwarf, and was earlier still *Jack
Prat*, which suggests some relationship with the
synonymous *dandiprat*, still used in dialect of an
undersized person or an urchin. There can be little
doubt that *dandy*, which has a great number of
figurative uses (see p. 20), is the pet-form of *Andrew*,
the special sense of fop, 'exquisite', being first
found on the Scottish Border.

Taking the European languages as a whole, the
dominant name is *John*. The boundless character
of this region of vocabulary is illustrated by a book [1]
now lying before me, the index to which enumerates
about a thousand figurative or punning uses of *Jean*
and his companion *Jeanne*, with their derivatives
and diminutives, almost 99 per cent being contemptuous. Some of these are not obvious on the
surface, e.g. *Tonton*, used at Verviers for a stupid
woman, is a baby-reduplication of the last syllable
of *Jeanneton*, double diminutive of *Jeanne*. A

---

[1] Cramer, Die Bedeutungsentwickelung von *Jean* im Franzö-
sischen (Giessen, 1931).

similar book might be written on the Dutch and German *Hans*, pet-form of *Johann*. *Hans* was, as late as Macaulay, a nickname for the Dutch nation, and *Hans in kelder* (Jack in the cellar) was vulgar English up to the 18th century for the unborn child.

On the whole *John* has, in English, preserved a little more dignity than *Jack*. *John Chinaman* is a shade more respectful than Defoe's *Jack Spaniard*. *John Company*, the old East India Company, is adapted from Dutch *Jan Kompanie*, a name given by the ' natives ', unable to visualize a corporation, to the Dutch East India Company and still to the Dutch government. With Shakespeare's *John a' dreams*—

> Yet I,
> A dull and muddy-mettled rascal, peak,
> Like John a' dreams, unpregnant of my cause,
> And can say nothing.
>
> (Hamlet, ii. 2),

we may compare French *Guillot le songeur*, ' a dreaming fellow, a dull sleepie logger-head ' (Cotgrave). *John Barleycorn*, as the personification of good malt liquor, occurs in a ballad of c. 1620, but his fame is chiefly due to Burns's song—

> Then let us toast John Barleycorn,
> Each man a glass in hand ;
> And may his great posterity
> Ne'er fail in old Scotland !

Though *John* and *Jack* predominate among personifications, nearly all familiar names have been similarly used at some time or other. *Peter grievous*, a lachrymose individual, belongs to the class of *simple Simon*, *Johnny raw*, etc. Most of the *Peter* combinations allude to *St. Peter* or to Rome, e.g. *peterman*, a fisherman, was in East Anglian use till quite recently, and a tax paid to the Holy See from Anglo-Saxon times till the Reformation was called *Peter's penny* or *Peter's pence*. These are intelligible, but why should *Peter* have meant a portmanteau in 18th century thieves' slang ? In the later 19th century *Johnny* [1] was for some time applied to the ' idle young man about town ', eventually becoming equivalent to chap, e.g. ' What does the inspector johnny want ? ' Somewhat more languid was *Algy*, flitting through Punch of the du Maurier period as a contrast to *'Arry*, the irrepressible cockney vulgarian, who first appears (in 1874) ' on 'orseback '. With *Algy* we may compare *Percy*, which had a tremendous vogue as a baptismal name about the middle of the 19th century and is still used in the United States of the typical young Englishman.

Just now there is a reaction in favour of the simple *John, Henry*, etc., or of good old names which were long out of fashion, such as *Roger, Michael, Peter* and *Anthony*. The hero of the modern novel is usually *Dick, Bill*, or *Jim*, the last being almost *de rigueur* in what has been called the ' thick ear ' school of romance, the central character of which is always the master of a devastating upper-cut, or, to use a younger and more expressive language, ' packs a mean wallop '. The more ornamental type has become derisive. During the War Punch depicted a non-com. of the old school

[1] *Johnny* is ' general Mediterranean ' for an Englishman.

vetoing the promotion of an intelligent private with
the decisive argument that the said private's name
was *Clarence*! I myself, when it was once my
privilege to assist a slightly elevated ' contemptible '
into a moving train, was effusively thanked
under the name of *'Arold*. More recently, when
I ventured to indicate to a fellow-traveller of
robust vocabulary that there was a lady in the
compartment, my hint was received with a readily
acquiescent ' Right O, *'Orace* ! '

Tom, *Dick* and *Harry* have stood for the populace
only since c. 1800. Prince Hal uses an earlier
variant—

> I am sworn brother to a leash of drawers ; and can call them
> all by their Christian names, as Tom, Dick and Francis.
>
> (1 Henry IV., ii. 4.)

Since much remoter times, shortened forms of
familiar names have been taken as representative
of the populace. Chaucer (D. 1356) contrasts
commoners like *Jakke* and *Rauf* [1] with *Sir Robert*
and *Sir Huwe*. Gower, in Vox Clamantis, enumerates the revolting peasants of 1381 as *Watte*
(Walter), *Thomme*, *Symme*, *Bette* (? Bartholomew,
? Bertram), *Gibbe* (Gilbert), *Hykke* (Richard), *Colle*
(Nicholas), *Geffe*, *Wille*, *Grigge* (Gregory), *Dawe*
(David), *Hobbe* (Robert), *Lorkyn* (Lawrence), *Hudde*
(? cf. Hudson), *Judde* (Jordan), *Tebbe* (Theobald)
and *Jakke*. Shakespeare, with the fine incongruity
of his age, makes Coriolanus (ii. 3) apostrophize the
Roman plebs as *Hob* and *Dick*. James I. rejects

[1] *Ralph* later rose in the world, but is used for the typical
charcoal-burner in the old story of Rauf Colyear (c. 1475).

with indignation the idea that ' *Jack* and *Tom* and *Will* and *Dick* shall meet and censure me and my government '. Minsheu (1617) describes the quintain as ' a sport at which *Jac* and *Tom*, *Dic*, *Hob* and *Will* strive for the gay garland '.

Hob, as a pet-form of *Robert*, is long obsolete, though it has supplied us with a group of surnames (*Hobbs*, *Hopkins*, etc.). It was once, like *Hodge*, a favourite name for the rustic,[1] and I fancy that some of the unexplained uses of the monosyllable *hob* are connected with the name, especially the peg or pin used as a mark at various games, e.g. at quoits. If the small white ball sent out as a mark at bowls is called *jack*, I do not see why the *hob* of quoits should not be of similar origin. Udall has *hoball* (see p. 146) for bumpkin, *Hobbinoll* is a rustic in Spenser's Shepheards Calendar, and the same *Hob* seems to have coloured *hobnail* and the mysterious *hobbledehoy*.[2] Finally, the expression to *hob-nob*, originally to drink together, has, to my mind, more to do with this familiar name than with the Shakespearean *hob-nob*, give or take, hit or miss, which is for earlier *hab-nab* (have, not have). The compound seems to express the hail-fellow-well-met attitude of those who are on Christian name terms, *Nob* being, like *Hob*, a pet-form of *Robert*. It will be remembered that the Bastard of Faulconbridge (King John, i. 1) describes his elder brother *Robert* as *Sir Nob*.

[1] The demon applications (p. 78) are later.
[2] First recorded from 1540, with a bewildering number of variants.

A certain number of names, as will already have been observed, are associated especially with domestic service. An early memory of the author's is that the school ' boots ' was always *John*, although he might protest that he had been christened *Henry* or *Archibald*. If we had studied Ben Jonson, we might have quoted—

> All constables are John to the king,
> Whate'er their names, be they Tony or Roger.
> (Tale of a Tub, iv. 2.)

John or *Thomas*, or the two combined, were regular nicknames for the 19th-century man-servant. In the 16th century we find *Tom* similarly used—

> When icicles hang by the wall,
>   And Dick the shepherd blows his nail,
>   And Tom bears logs within the hall . . .
>   (Love's Labour's Lost, v. 2),

and *Tom* and *Tib* [1] (i.e. *Isabel*) were rival personifications of *Jack* and *Jill*. *Tomboy* was an unruly boy before becoming a boisterous girl, and the wandering lunatic was *Tom o' Bedlam* (see pp. 68, 113). More humorous than *Thomas*, the footman, is *Jeames*, the Scottish form of *James*, the vowel sound of which is considered vastly diverting, though nobody is ever moved to hilarity by *Jean*, the Scottish form of *Jane*.

Tusser [2] is our great authority for this nomenclature. He seems unable to visualize characters

---

[1] Also a goose, *Tib of the buttery*, and a favourite cat. For *Tib's eve* see p. 120 It may be noted, however, that a Saint Tibba is actually mentioned in the Anglo-Saxon Chronicle.

[2] In his Hundreth Good Pointes of Husbandrie (1557).

unless personified and he even views plants in the same way—

> Go into thy hop-yard, for now it is time
> To teach Robin Hop on his pole how to climb.

The man and maid are *Jack* and *Bess*, or *Hob* and *Margery*—

> To raise betimes the lubberly,
> Both snorting (i.e. snoring) Hob and Margery—

or *Jankin* and *Jennykin*, *Jack* and *Gill*, *Jack* and *Joan*. An idler is *Hob Grouthead*, a slattern *Gill Laggoose*. The predatory tramp is *Hew Makeshift* and his equally predatory companion is *Gillet*. A careless housewife is *Gillian Spendall*, the dairy-maid is usually *Ciss* or *Cisley* (i.e. *Cecilia*)—

> When Tom came home from labour,
> And Ciss from milking rose.
>
> (Bishop Corbet),

and a general term for a maid is *Nan* (*Anne*)—

> Such mistress, such Nan;
> Such master, such man.

Such customs are persistent. With Chaucer's *Malkin* (p. 86) we may compare the 19th-century *Mary Ann*, or the modern American *Biddy* (i.e. *Bridget*) for an Irish ' help '.

There are a few examples of less abbreviated names. *Andrew*, once a stock name for a gentleman's servant, survives in *Merry Andrew*, the conjurer's assistant. Congreve links him with *Abigail*—

' I am brought to fine uses, to become a botcher of second-hand marriages between Abigails and Andrews '.

(Way of the World, v. 1.)

Abigail, in this sense, dates from Beaumont and Fletcher's Scornful Lady, in which a 'waiting gentlewoman' so called plays an important rôle, her name perhaps suggested by the repetition of 'thine handmaid' in 1 Samuel xxv. 24 sqq. Another name for the conjurer's assistant was *zany*, which is Italian *Zanni*, a dialect pet-form of *Giovanni* (John)—

> He's like the zany to a tumbler,
> That tries tricks after him to make men laugh.
> (Ben Jonson, Every Man out of his Humour, iv. 1.)

He was also called *Mr. Merriman*, *Merry Andrew* (v.s.) and *Jack Pudding*. With the latter we may compare the synonymous French *Jean Potage*, Dutch *Hanssop*, and German *Hanswurst* (Jack sausage).

Finally we have that etymological problem the *merry grig*. From the early 16th century we find this description of a 'good fellow' running parallel with *merry Greek*, and the probability is that the latter (which makes no particular sense) is a corruption of the former. *Grig* is used in dialect of various small animals, but the *grig*, a cricket, given by some dialect glossaries, appears to be an unwarranted inference from the phrase 'as merry as a cricket'. This association has coloured the later meaning of the *merry grig*, who, for the 16th century, was a jovial blade, boon companion. Now *Gregory* was a common Middle English name, familiarly shortened to *Grig* (see p. 92). It was also in early use, like some of the other names in this chapter, for a man-servant, e.g. in Romeo and Juliet and the Taming of the Shrew. Though now always with *merry*, the word often occurs earlier alone, apparently in the sense of boon companion. Therefore I suggest, with all humility, that we may have here one more example of a personal name taken as a type. Why *Gregory*[1] ? Well, why *Gaultier* in *bon Gaultier* (p. 83, n. 1) ? Why *Will o' the wisp* (p. 73) ? Why *Old Nick* (p. 71) ? Who gave the name *Phineas* to the wooden Highlander (one of my earliest memories) which is now the inalienable property of University College, London ? It may be noted that *Grégoire* occurs in French slang for a toper, frequently riming with *boire* in drinking-songs of the 16th century ; also that *Gregory* is used (in 1599) of a ' gallant ' by Massinger, who has ' my *Gregories* ', i.e. my gay friends, in a context similar to that in which Brome (in 1638) has ' my *grigs* '. *Gregorians* were still a convivial society in the 18th century, and the following lines from Crabbe are suggestive—

> Griggs and Gregorians here their meetings hold ;
> Convivial sects and ' bucks ' alert and bold.
> (The Borough, x. 349.)

---

[1] A reader suggests a natural connection with the New Testament Greek *grēgorein*, to keep awake.

CHAPTER VIII

BOYCOTT & CO.

THE present year (1932) is the centenary of the birth of *Charles Cunningham Boycott*, once agent for Lord Erne's estates in Co. Mayo. His persecution, at the instigation of the Irish Land League, resulted in a verb which has been adopted in some form or other by nearly every European language. It is said to have first appeared in print in the Freeman's Journal report of a speech made at Maam in Connemara by Mr. William O'Malley, M.P., in 1880. At any rate, this gentleman laid claim to the doubtful honour, when the ' jubilee ' of the word in 1930 led to a newspaper discussion of its origin. The jubilee of *boycott* almost coincided with the centenary of *burke*, which seems to have been spontaneously coined by the Edinburgh mob—

As soon as the executioner proceeded to his duty, the cries of ' Burke him, burke him—give him no rope ' were vociferated.
(Times, Feb. 2, 1829.)

William Burke, with his confederate Hare, had suffocated a number of people in order to dispose of their bodies to the anatomist Robert Knox, whose dealings with the resurrectionists [1]

[1] ' We have heard that, owing to the strictness with which the resurrection-men have been watched lately, and the consequent

were conducted on the principle of 'no questions asked'.

Originally used in reference to actual smothering, the word soon acquired the sense of metaphorically stifling, hushing up, etc. It has not attained the international fame of *boycott*, but it is interesting to note that both words, with their contrasted passive and active origins, are ultimately connected with Ireland, for Burke and Hare were immigrants from the *Emerald Isle*.[1] One *Bishop*, who, fired with the same scientific ardour as *Burke*, murdered a boy at Bethnal Green in 1831, has been less fortunate, though his name survived as a verb for some thirty years—

> Away the rogue ran
> To that self-same unprincipled seafaring man ;
> In his ear whisper'd low. . . . Bully Gaussen said, ' Done !
> I burk'd the papa, now I'll bishop the son.'
> (' Ingoldsby,' Some Account of a New Play.)

Another verb *bishop*, to file down the teeth of an old horse so as to make it appear young, probably commemorates some horse-dealer of the early 18th century. The word is still in use.

As a rule it is the victim whose name is immortalized. An early example is *coventry*, to slit the nose, for which the Oxford Dictionary has a quotation dated 1704. In 1670, *Sir John Coventry* was waylaid by ruffians who slit his nose as a punish-

deficient supply of subjects, some of the lecturers on anatomy in the West End have been unable to go on with their lectures ' (Times, Nov. 16, 1828).

[1] First so called, towards the end of the 18th century, by William Drennan, an Irish poet.

ment for his criticism of Charles II.'s morals.   This
outrage led to the passing of the Coventry Act
against mutilation.   In 1678, *Sir Edmund Berry
Godfrey*, who was considered the best justice of the
peace in England, received the depositions of Titus
Oates.   His murder, a month later, is one of the
great mysteries of criminal history.   In 1685, John
Crowne introduced his name into a play—' Don't
throttle me, don't godfrey me ' (Sir Courtly Nice,[1]
ii. 2).   The Oxford Dictionary does not record the
verb to *godfrey*, but it has copious examples, from
1689 to 1888, of *dewitt*, ' a bloody word, but too well
understood ' (Archbishop Sancroft).   In 1672, *John*
and *Cornelius de Witt*, political opponents of William
of Orange (afterwards William III. of England),
were, as readers of La Tulipe Noire will remember,
butchered by the mob.   A pamphlet of 1695
describes the ' Dewitting of Glencoe ', and, in 1699,
Tom Brown, of *Dr. Fell*[2] fame, notes that, when a
town-councillor of Amsterdam proposed to close the
famous Long Cellar, he 'was like to be de-witted
by the mob '.   More complicated is the history of
the American *gerrymander*, to ' manipulate ' elec-
tions.   *Elbridge Gerry*, governor of Massachusetts
in the early 19th century, arranged electoral divisions
with a view to favouring his own party.   The
fantastic shape of one of these divisions on the map

[1] For this name cf. p. 139.

[2] *John Fell*, Dean of Christ Church, Oxford, subject of an
adaptation by Tom Brown, when an undergraduate, of Martial's
Epigram (i. 33)—

> Non amo te, Sabidi, nec possum dicere quare ;
> Hoc tantum possum dicere, non amo te.

suggested to a painter a *salamander*, improved by a journalist into *gerrymander*. This somehow suggests *bunkum*, earlier *buncombe*, which does not really belong here. The Congress member for *Buncombe*, in North Carolina, is said to have excused himself for a futile contribution to debate by explaining that he was ' making a speech for Buncombe '—

All over America every place likes to hear of its member of Congress and see their speeches ; and if they don't, they send a piece to the paper, inquirin' if their member's died a natural death or was skivered with a bowie knife, for they hante seen his speeches lately and his friends are anxious to know his fate. Our free and enlightened citizens don't approbate silent members. So every feller, in bounden duty, talks, and talks big too, and the smaller the state, the louder, bigger and fiercer its members talk. Well, when a crittur talks for talk sake, jist to have a speech in the paper to send to home, and not for any other airthly puppus but electioneering, our folks call it ' bunkum '.

(' Sam Slick '.)

The word is now commonly shortened to *bunk*, whence the verb *debunk*, used by those of iconoclastic tendencies. Shakespeare Debunked is the title of a book recently published in America. *Bunkum* is akin to *blarney*, a quality acquired by kissing a particular stone at *Blarney Castle*, near Cork.

Next to *boycott*, the most international verb of this class is *lynch* (whence French *lyncher*, German *lynchen*, Italian *linciare*). Its origin is very uncertain. The etymology usually given is from ' *Charles Lynch*, a Virginia justice of the peace, who jailed many loyalists in 1780 without warrant in law ' (Mencken, The American Language), and the earlier form *Lynch's law* seems to point to a personal

origin. But Mr. Albert Matthews, who has done
so much valuable work in the by-ways of word-
history, finds no evidence for this theory. It is
known that *Lynche's Creek*, in S. Carolina, was, as
early as 1768, a meeting-place of the Regulators,
or amateur administrators of criminal justice, so
that the term may be really of local origin. If so,
Lynch Law belongs to the same class as the historic
Jeddart or *Jedwood* [1] *justice*, i.e. trial after execution,
and *Lydford Law*.[2] The latter, from *Lydford* (Dart-
moor), is connected with a Stannaries (i.e. tin-
mining) Court of summary jurisdiction and is mentioned in Langland's [3] Richard the Redeless (1399).
This is historical, but the origins of such expressions
are generally obscured by ' anecdotic ' etymology.
An example is *Scarborough warning*, sometimes
defined as ' a word and a blow, and the blow first '.
This is connected by Fuller with the surprise land-
ing, in 1557, of the rebel Thomas Stafford ; but the
Oxford Dictionary, passing like an imperturbable
steam-roller over the sand-castles of the early etymologists, finds a record for 1546.[4] So the association
of the *warning* with *Scarborough* remains as obscure

---

[1] From *Jedburgh*, in Roxburghshire, whence also Scott's
Jedwood axe.

[2] Cf. *Halifax* (p. 150).

[3] Langland is also our earliest authority (Piers Plowman,
A.x. 189) for the *Dunmow flitch* as a reward for harmonious
married life. The award is said to have been established in
1244 at Dunmow, Essex, by Robert Fitzwalter, Lord of Dunmow and leader of the barons who forced John to sign the Great
Charter.

[4] For a still better example of the etymological ' So near and
yet so far ' see my Adjectives and Other Words, p. 51.

as that of the famous *curse* with *Sedgley* (Stafford-shire)—

A Sedgley curse light on him ; which is, Pedro, ' The fiend ride through him booted and spurred, with a scythe at his back.'
                                   (Fletcher, Woman's Prize, v. 2.)

Stafford court or *law* is a crude pun (see p. 151). Cotgrave has ' *Il a esté au festin de Martin baston*,[1] he hath had a triall in Stafford Court.'

A limited number of geographical names have joined the company of *boycott* and *burke*. Did not Lord Fisher, in pre-War days, suggest to King Edward that he should be allowed to *Copenhagen* the growing German fleet ? The allusion was to our illegal seizure, in 1807, of the Danish fleet in order to prevent its being used against us by Napoleon. The most familiar perhaps is *shanghai*, to ' dope ' seamen and put them on board in a state of insensibility, a practice attributed to the Chinese port of *Shang-Hai*, but apparently most efficiently exercised at San Francisco. At any rate the word is of American origin. Of much greater antiquity is the obsolete *barbadose*, which, under the Common-wealth, meant to transport prisoners to *Barbados*. During the South African War incompetent officers were sometimes *stellenbosched*, i.e. relegated to a position where they could do no harm. *Stellenbosch*, in Cape Colony, is said to have been a place of retirement for unsuccessful commanders during the Kaffir wars. This would make it a parallel to French *limoger*, used during the World War of

[1] French *Martin-bâton*, the disciplinary stick, illustrates the popular love of personification especially discussed in chapter iv.

sending similar cases to *Limoges*. But the explanation is of late date and unsupported by evidence.
As early as 1797, Lady Anne Barnard, author of
Auld Robin Gray, describes *Stellenbosch*, in her South
African Journal, as a quiet and pleasant place
serving only as 'the asylum for old age', which
suggests that the original witticism may have been
of the *go to Bath* type, advice given to those showing signs of weakness, especially mental ! It is open
to any writer to add to this class of words. When
Mr. Kipling makes the Man who would be King
lament that there are few regions left which two
strong men can *Sa-ra-wak*, he is alluding to the
sort of sovereignty set up in 1841 at *Sarawak*, in
Borneo, by 'Rajah Brooke', whose line still holds
sway there.

It will have been noticed that the majority of
the words mentioned so far have a brutal significance.
Some of them go to confirm Halifax's dictum that
'the angry buzz of a multitude is one of the bloodiest
noises in the world'. We may compare the slogan
(to use the fashionable word) *Give him Camborne*,
which may occasionally be heard in Cornwall, when
civil dudgeon grows high. It usually connotes the
hammering into insensibility of some imprudently
vocal Tory by a dozen or so political thinkers of
a more advanced school. This method of making
the world safe for democracy is by no means con-
fined to Cornwall, but I cannot remember any
similar use of a place-name elsewhere, though *Lime-
house*, from a speech made in that favoured locality
by Mr. Lloyd George, before he mellowed, is some-

times used of political invective that transcends the bounds of good taste. *Whitechapel*, potting one's opponent at billiards or leading from a single card at whist, is a slur on another London suburb.

The ' Camborne ' psychology of the *bête humaine* is revealed in the records of the various ' captains ' in whom mob valour has been personified in the past. We have *Captain Ludd*, machine-breaker in the Midlands (1811–16), *Captain Swing*, rick-burner in Kent (1830–32), *Captain Moonlight*, nocturnal attacker of Irish landlords (c. 1880), successor to the *Molly Maguires* of 1843, who made their visits in female attire. One of the earliest of such pseudonyms is *Jack Straw*, assumed as a typical peasant name by a leader in the Peasant Revolt of 1381, whose exploits were still fresh in Chaucer's memory five years later—

> So hydous was the noys, *a benedicitee* !
> Certes, ne Jakke Straw and his meynee
> Ne made never shoutes half as shrille.
>
> (B. 4583.)

Among the linguistic phenomena which bring about the creation of new words is one which philologists call back-formation. This is best explained by examples. From the old word *ped*, basket, still current in East Anglia, was formed *pedder*, an itinerant dealer, a form found in Wyclif. This was later altered to *peddler*, just as *tinker* has become, in some dialects, *tinkler*. As a *meddler* is one who *meddles*, the popular mind conceived that a *pedlar* must be one who *peddles*, and thus a new verb came into existence some centuries later than the noun

H

which gave birth to it. Similarly from *burglar* has been evolved the verb *burgle*. We have literary authority for the fact that—

> When the enterprising burglar's not a burgling . . . ,
> He loves to hear the little brook a-gurgling.
> (Gilbert, Pirates of Penzance),

and humorists occasionally describe the activities of the *butler* as *buttling*. The American language is constantly creating new verbs by shortening, e.g. to *peeve*, *enthuse*, *resurrect*, and even to *approbate* (p. 101).

More complicated is the history of *grovel*, which, so far as records go, was coined (like most of the English language) by Shakespeare—

> What seest thou there ? King Henry's diadem,
> Enchased with all the honours of the world ?
> If so, gaze on and grovel on thy face,
> Until thy head be circled with the same.
> (1 Henry VI., i. 2.)

The word is inferred from the old adverb *grovelling*, face downwards, erroneously taken as a present participle. The same adverbial ending appears in *sideling* (= *sidelong*), from which the 17th century formed the verb to *sidle*. The more modern *darkle*, from the old adverb *darkling*, appears to have been coined by Byron as a contrasted rime to *sparkle*.

It is natural that proper names ending in *-ing* should occasionally be treated in the same way. It was J. K. Stephen who sang of a future age 'When the Rudyards cease from Kipling and the Haggards Ride no more'. In 1863 *William Banting*, a London undertaker, who, after enduring for many years 'le martyre de l'obèse', had reduced his weight by attention to diet, published A Letter on Corpulence. His 'system of abstaining' from certain foods was called *banting* and those who followed it were said to *bant*, a word once quite familiar but now seldom heard. May 17, 1900, saw the relief of *Mafeking*, a South African town besieged by the Boers and defended by Sir R. Baden Powell, of Boy Scout fame. On May 22, the now defunct Pall-Mall Gazette advised Cape Town to *maffick*, 'if we may coin a word'.

In 1803 Lamb's friend James Kenney produced in London a very successful farce called Raising the Wind. The chief character in the piece was a swindling rogue called *Jeremy Diddler*. The same instinct which makes us regard a *burglar* as one who *burgles* was responsible for the feeling that a *Diddler* must be one who *diddles*. Hence the creation of a new verb, which was at once adopted by London slang and spread rapidly to every part of England and Scotland. We do not know what led Kenney to use the name *Diddler*. He may have known the rare 16th-century *duddle*, to confuse, which is possibly related to Anglo-Saxon *dyderian*, but he is solely responsible for supplying the language with *diddle*.

So far we have dealt especially with words illustrating the unique English power of turning a noun into a verb. It will be remembered that Rogue Riderhood (Our Mutual Friend) condemned *poll-parotting*. Our language, like others, can form verbs from proper names by means of the Greek suffix *-ize, -ise.*[1] The Greeks themselves coined *Hellēnizein,* to imitate the Greeks, speak Greek, *Mēdizein,* to side with the Medes, and *Philippizein*—

The first new-coined word that I know of was struck by Demosthenes, who, having heard that King Philip of Macedon had bribed the oracle in order to dispirit the Athenians, accused the priestess of Philippizing.

(Pegge, Anecdotes.)

It would be wearisome to enumerate all the verbs in *-ize* that have to do with scientific and industrial processes. Examples are *harveyize,* from *H. A. Harvey,* of New Jersey, who, in 1888, patented in England a method of hardening armour-plate; *kyanize,* to impregnate timber with preservatives, a process patented in 1832 by *J. H. Kyan; mercerize,* from *John Mercer,* an Accrington dyer, who patented, in 1850, a new way of treating textiles and made many other discoveries in connection with his industry. *Pasteurize,* to sterilize, is a process invented by *Louis Pasteur* (+ 1895). Much older is *Mithridatize,* to render immune to poison, from *Mithridates,* King of Pontus (1st century B.C.), who traditionally dosed himself regularly for this purpose. Tennyson revived the 16th-century *gorgonize,* to petrify with a baleful glance, when Maud's brother—

Curving a contumelious lip,
Gorgonized me from head to foot
With a stony British stare,

---

[1] Along with these go the *-ists* and *-isms,* but the infinite variety of early Christian sects, modern nonconformist bodies, and offshoots from the parent stem of socialism makes the subject too formidable for treatment.

and C.L.G., in Punch, has recently perpetrated a
new formation—

> Shall we then, awed by scientific swipes,
> Meekly revert to our ancestral types,
> And, having all carnivorous food tabooed,
> Nebuchadnezzarize our daily food ?

More ' literary ' is *grangerize*, to improve a book
by the insertion of suitable illustrations taken from
other sources. The verb is derived from *James
Granger*, who published, in 1769, a Biographical
History of England with blank pages for the addition
of illustrative engravings. Most famous of all is
bowdlerize. In 1818 *Thomas Bowdler* published an
expurgated Family Shakespeare which could ' with
propriety be read aloud in a family '. Eight years
later, the Observer for December 31, 1826, mentions
it with approval under the heading ' Appropriate
Xmas Presents ', quoting the Edinburgh Review's
opinion that ' it requires nothing more than a
notice to bring this very meritorious publication
into general circulation '. Poor *Bowdler* has become,
rather unjustly, a kind of male *Mrs. Grundy*. After
all, the Shakespeare that boys and girls ' do ' at
school is still strictly, and very rightly, *bowdlerized*.
With this verb we may compare the German
ballhornisieren or *verballhornen*, to ruin a book by
' improvements ', after the manner of *Johann Ball-
horn*, a Lübeck printer of the 16th century. The
French *berquinade*, an insipid, goody-goody book,
is derived from *Arnaud Berquin*, an 18th-century
author of moral tales for children. *Marivaudage* is
applied to a rather exaggerated and elaborate type

of amorous gallantry exemplified in the delightful comedies of *Marivaux* (1688–1765).

The derivation of verbs in *-ize* from geographical words is a very natural process. One of the most barbarous is *westernize*, for which *occidentalize* has also been used. Often, as in some of the Greek examples quoted on p. 108, to which we may add *Scythizein*, to behave, especially drink, like a Scythian, such words have an acid flavour. *Americanize* was originally opprobrious. *Prussianize* is generally connected with the government of Alsace-Lorraine after the cession of the provinces to Germany in 1871. In the 16th century Henri Estienne bitterly satirized the *français italianisé* spoken by courtiers. New specimens are constantly being coined. The Observer of May 11, 1919, prophesied that the Treaty of Versailles would *balkanize* three-fourths of Europe, ' if we may coin the word,' and *balkaniser* is now accepted French. When, at the conclusion of the World War, Britain and France disagreed on their Turkish policy, the French troops were withdrawn from *Chanak*, on the south side of the Dardanelles, which gave rise to the French verb *chanaker*, to leave an ally in the lurch. Some French journalist, however, feared that we, being left in sole possession, might proceed to *gibraltariser* the Straits !

The last two are still-born nonce-words, but *Poplarity* and *Poplarize*, alluding to the lavish distribution of the ratepayers' money by the *Poplar* Board of Guardians in 1921, have probably more vitality. The Oxford Dictionary does not register the verb to *grimthorpe* or the noun *mervousness*. The former, coined by the Athenaeum, in 1892, to describe *Lord Grimthorpe's* much criticized restoration of St. Albans Abbey, is occasionally used by architects. *Mervousness* was a state of mind attributed by the then (1882) Duke of Argyll to Lord Roberts, who had warned the Government of Russia's designs on *Merv* in Turkestan. The Russians took the town the next year.

Somewhat akin to the matter contained in this chapter is the use of historic names to represent types of physique or character. Here, in spite of our enlightenment, we cannot get away from the Bible and the ancients. A hunter is still a *Nimrod* (Genesis x. 9), a giant a *son of Anak* (Deuteronomy ix. 2), and James I. was called, perhaps half-ironically, the British *Solomon*, a name borne before him by Henry VII. and by more than one professional fool ! With *Jehu*, a coachman [1] (2 Kings ix. 20), we may compare the corresponding use in French of *Automédon*, the charioteer of Achilles. The politician in search of a ' better 'ole ' is an *Adullamite* [2] (1 Samuel xxii. 2), and various female types are represented by *Magdalen*, with its old pronunciation *maudlin*, *Delilah* and *Jezebel*, the last of whom is

[1] The origin of *jarvey*, 18th-century *jarvis*, is uncertain. According to some it is an allusion to *St. Gervase*, whose attribute is a whip. There is also a tradition that *Jarvis* was a hackney-coachman who was hanged, which would make it a parallel to the synonymous French *Collignon*, from the name of a cabby who murdered his fare.

[2] This sense was fixed in 1866, by John Bright, in reference to a group which had seceded from the Liberal party to form a ' cave ', but the word had been similarly used as early as 1834.

chiefly remembered for having painted her face
just before her defenestration.[1] From *Job* we
have French *jobard*, a patient ninny, and our own
jobation, the kind of lecture addressed to Job by
his comforters, which in rustic English becomes
jawbation. With German *Hiobspost*, bad news, cf.
Uriasbrief (2 Sam. xi. 14), letter destructive to its
bearer. *Moloch*, a Canaanitish idol identical with
Hebrew *melek*, king, owes his fame especially to
Milton. His name is often used of a merciless all-
devouring force, just as we erroneously attribute to
Juggernaut, the idol drawn in procession at Orissa,
the wholesale crushing of fanatical pilgrims, who
are fabled to have cast themselves beneath his
car.

The editors of the Oxford Dictionary have recently
asked for early examples of the interjectional
Jehoshaphat, whether ' jumping ' or otherwise. The
popularity of this minor personage is due to the
euphemistic substitution of his name for another
more sacred. Of similar origin are *gee-whittakers*,
gee-whiz, *Christ-opher*, *jiminy* or *gemini* (German
jemine, contraction of *Jesu Domine*), *criminy*, *crikey*,
lawks-a-mercy, *by gosh*, *golly*, etc. The same avoid-
ance of blasphemy appears in the more recent
Americanisms ' What the *Sam Hill* ? ' and ' for the
love of *Mike* '.

The fame of *Daniel*, apart from the lions' den
episode, comes from the youthful *Daniel* of the

[1] This curious piece of pedantry was first used in connection
with the throwing out of window of the Imperial commissioners
Slawata and Martinitz at Prague (May 23, 1618), the beginning
of the Thirty Years War.

Apocrypha, who caused Susanna to be discharged without a stain on her character—

> A Daniel come to judgment! yea, a Daniel!
> O wise young judge, how do I honour thee!
> (Merchant of Venice, iv. 1.)

The Apocrypha may also be the ultimate source of the *Danse Macabre* or Dance of Death, which is called *Chorea Machabaeorum* in the 15th century, but the history of this word, though much discussed, has not yet been clearly traced.

To Biblical geography we owe, among other words, *bedlam*, from the London lunatic asylum known as *Bethlehem Hospital*, first founded in 1247, *Armageddon* (Revelation xvi. 16), apparently the mount of *Megiddo* (Judges v. 19), which was used of the anticipated World War many years before it began, and the unexplained ' go to *Jericho* '. There are plenty of conjectures for *Jericho*, but they are hardly to be taken more seriously than ' Ingoldsby's ' crusading reminiscence—

His (the Baron of Sheppey's) kick was tremendous, and when he had his boots on, would,—to use an expression of his own, which he had picked up in the holy wars,—send a man ' from Jericho to June '.

(Grey Dolphin.)

Gehenna is a late Greek form of the valley of *Hinnom*, where children were sacrificed to Baal and Moloch (Jeremiah xix.) ; cf. Arabic *Jehannum*. Two Biblical place-names are used in a puzzling way, viz. *galilee*, a cathedral porch at Durham and elsewhere, and the French *capharnäum*, a crowded lumber-room, for both of which it is possible, but hardly profitable, to guess reasons.

A Board of Education report on the teaching of English, which attracted much attention in 1921, says, ' At the present time the Bible is probably less widely read and less directly influential in our life and literature than it has been at any time since the Reformation.' After a couple more generations of democratic control it is likely that young England will require elucidatory notes for *Egyptian darkness* or the *Massacre of the Innocents*, and that allusions to *Rechabites* (Jeremiah xxxv.) and *Laodiceans* (Revelation iii. 15), *Ichabod* (1 Samuel iv. 21) and *Mizpah* (Genesis xxxi. 49) will be regarded as too recondite for the modern mind.

The Greeks and Romans, like the Scriptures, have contributed to our gallery of typical characters to an extent which is not even approached by the figures of later European history. Even the best noses are classified as *Greek* or *Roman*, artistic or masterful. Pip opined that ' the Romans must have aggravated one another very much with their noses ' (Great Expectations, ch. iv). We may describe a man as the Napoleon of Wall Street or of the bun-trade, but we do not call him Napoleon *tout court*, in the way in which we call a misanthrope a *Timon* or a wise law-giver a *Justinian*. When we want a word expressive of severe legislation, we remember *Draco*, archon of Athens (621 B.C.), whose laws were said to be written in blood, and a loud voice inevitably suggests *Stentor*, herald of the Greek host before Troy. No dynastic adjective, not even *Elizabethan* or *Victorian*, has quite the majesty of *Augustan*,[1] the age when the Emperor and his friend Maecenas were the patrons of Horace and Virgil.

An invective speech is still a *philippic*, as when Demosthenes urged his countrymen to arm themselves against *Philip of Macedonia*, a savage whose habits are clearly indicated in the expression ' to appeal from *Philip drunk* to *Philip sober* '. To his son we ultimately owe the *alexandrine*, the metre of an Old French poem on *Alexandre le Grand*. This conqueror, called in the East *Iskander*, gave his name to almost as many places as Queen Victoria. One of them is *Iskanderun*, a port of Syria, whence *scanderoon*, a breed of carrier pigeons said to have been used originally for transmitting news of the arrival of ships to the merchants of Aleppo.   *Pyrrhic victory*, i.e. one gained at too great cost, celebrates the battle of Asculum (279 B.C.), where *Pyrrhus*, king of Epirus, beat the Romans.

A very rich man is either a *Croesus*, last king of Lydia (6th century B.C.), or a *Midas*, the fabulous king of Phrygia, whose touch turned everything to gold.   To get rid of this embarrassing habit Midas bathed in the river *Pactolus*, which ever after ran gold in its waters. We still use *Gordian knot*, tied by *Gordius*, king of Gordium, and ' untied ' by Alexander with his sword, for a difficult problem, and *sword of Damocles* for an imminent but unsuspected danger, such as threatened *Damocles*, when

[1] The *Augustan Confession* was drawn up (1530) by Luther and Melanchthon at *Augsburg*, one of the many towns named from the Emperor.

feasted by Dionysius of Syracuse. The tomb of *Mausolus*, King of Caria (4th century B.C.), was one of the Seven Wonders of the World, and, when we describe a man as a *colossus*, we think of the *Colossus* fabled to bestride the port of Rhodes.

One of the greatest of the Greeks has been maligned by posterity, viz. the Athenian philosopher *Epicurus*, who taught that happiness was the *summum bonum*—

> Who can but pity the virtuous Epicurus, who is commonly conceived to have placed his chief felicity in pleasure and sensual delights and hath therefore left an infamous name behind him ?
>
> (Sir Thomas Browne.)

Another misuse of a Greek philosopher's name is in *Platonic love*, an ideal that sprang up in the Italian academies of the Renaissance. Possibly no Greek name was for centuries so familiar in England as that of *Euclid*, the Alexandrian mathematician (c. 300 B.C.), who is now, I understand, superseded. I remember that, when I first went to school at the age of seven, I imagined for some time that *euclid* was a difficult language studied by big boys for whom Latin and Greek had no more secrets.

The Roman contribution is less interesting than the Greek, though many words are derived from the name of the greatest man of antiquity, who also supplied Germany and Russia with their Imperial titles. The Greek *Thespis*, traditional founder of tragedy, is commemorated in the *Thespian* (theatrical) *Club*, but when we wish to extol an English actor we call him a *Roscius*, from the Roman tragedian (+ 62 B.C.). An odd degradation of a famous Roman name is the Italian *cicerone*, a prattling guide. Still more offensive is the French *vespasienne*, a public lavatory, from the name of the Emperor *Vespasian*, who levied a tax on such conveniences. One of the most generally used of all words connected with Roman history is *Fabian*, from *Fabius Maximus*, who, appointed Dictator after the Trasimene disaster (217 B.C.), adopted such cautious tactics that he was nick-named the Cunctator, i.e. the delayer. The *Fabian Society* was founded in 1884 for the ' gradual ' conversion of the nation to socialism.

As already suggested, the number of more modern names used in this way is comparatively small. One thinks of *Bayard*,[1] the French knight *sans peur et sans reproche*, who fell at Romagnano in 1524, of *Machiavelli* of Florence (+ 1527), whose work Il Principe was supposed to inculcate maxims of unscrupulous statesmanship, and of *James Crichton*, the gifted young Scot, surnamed (by Urquhart) the *Admirable*, who was killed in a brawl at Mantua c. 1585. In this region of words, as elsewhere, one notices how the unimportant has sometimes survived. Few people would now remember *John Fell*, dean of Christ Church and bishop of Oxford (+ 1686), but for Tom Brown's undergraduate rendering of Martial's epigram (p. 100, n. 2). *According to Cocker* immortalizes *Edward Cocker*, writing-master and arithmetician (+ 1675). America prefers *according*

---

[1] *Bayard*, the horse, is a different name. It is Old French for bay and was borne especially by the long-backed steed which carried the four sons of Aymon. *Bayard of ten toes* is old slang for *Shanks's mare*.

to Hoyle, from *Edward Hoyle* (+ 1769), writer on card-games and chess. *Namby-pamby* was the nickname of *Ambrose Phillips* (+ 1749), author of poetic addresses to the infant nobility. A stale joke is still a *Joe Miller*, from a jest-book published in 1739 under the name of a recently deceased comedian, and *Jack Ketch* (+ 1686), who made such a mangling business of Monmouth's execution, became the soubriquet of the common hangman.

CHAPTER IX

A THRUSH in my garden, steadily repeating a chirrup which rustics sometimes interpret as 'pretty Dick', inspires the timid conjecture that this may be the origin of *dicky bird*. Or is *Dicky* just an accidental and arbitrary choice? Like nearly every familiar Christian name, the pet-form of *Richard* has many meanings in colloquial speech, some apparently due to the popular tendency to personify, others illustrating the equally popular tendency to twist a common noun into a form suggesting a personal name. Besides being applied to a bird, *dicky* means, in colloquial or dialect speech, a jackass, an under-petticoat, a bib, apron, overall, etc., a detachable shirt-front, and part of a vehicle. As an adjective it means shaky, queer, out of sorts. The shorter *Dick*, companion of *Tom* and *Harry*, is used by Shakespeare for chap, fellow. At a still earlier date a dangerous ruffian was called alliteratively a *desperate Dick*, while *dirty Dick* is still a familiar description of the unwashed. A Liverpool man is *Dicky Sam*,[1] just as a Cornishman is *cousin*[1]

---

[1] The first is probably from the old Lancashire way of indicating parentage (*Dick o' Sam's*); the second perhaps alludes to the Celtic practice of tracing remote relationships; cf. French *cousin à la mode de Bretagne*, a distant kinsman.

Jack. The name is also given to various plants and birds, e.g. *Dick dunnock*, the hedge-sparrow, and to the *will o' the wisp* (p. 74). But some senses exemplify assimilation of other words to a familiar name, e.g. in *up to dick* and to *take one's dick*, it is short for *declaration* ; in the archaic sense of fine words, flowery speech, it is for *dictionary* ; and in modern slang it is an arbitrary shortening of *detective*. ' In the reign of *Queen Dick* ' was formerly used for never, like the Latin *ad calendas Graecas* (because the Greeks had no *Calends*), our rustic *latter Lammas* [1] and *Tib's eve* (see p. 94), the French *semaine des quatre jeudis*, and the Dutch *een blaauwe maandag*, once in a blue moon.

Revenons à nos oiseaux. A number of our more homely birds are so commonly decorated with pet names that we hardly speak of them otherwise. Such are *jackdaw, tomtit, magpie, robin redbreast*. With these we may put *jenny wren* and *poll parrot*, the latter a mixture of the sexes, since *parrot* is French *pierrot*, a diminutive of *Pierre*, applied in modern French to the sparrow. These are perhaps the most familiar, but there is hardly a bird known to the country-side which does not bear in rustic dialect a variety of similar names, e.g. the pied wagtail is called *Molly wash-dish* and *Peggy dish-washer*, the moor-hen is *Kitty coot*, the hedge-sparrow *Betty*, the missel-thrush *Charlie-cock*. In Lincolnshire a gosling is *Gib*, i.e. *Gilbert*, and in the Craven dialect the owl is *Jenny hullett* (see p. 126), and so

---

[1] Harvest festival, ' loaf-mass ' (Aug. 1).

ad infinitum. This prefixing of a pet name seems to be a specially English practice, though the application of personal names to birds is common enough in other languages, e.g. in French the starling is sometimes called *sansonnet*, i.e. little Samson, and the magpie *jacquette* or *margot*. The only common English example of the actual replacement of the bird-name by a nickname is *robin*, which is found as early as the 16th century, while *Robin redbreast* is recorded in the 15th.

Except for *robin* the appellations mentioned above are, so far as documentary evidence goes, of comparatively recent date, but we have a few early examples which belong to the same age as the curious collection of animal names discussed in connection with *Reynard the Fox* (p. 131) and which apparently belong to some prehistoric ' beast-epic '.[1] *Mallard*, the wild drake, is identical with French *malart*, found already in the 12th century, and the Middle English variant *mawdelard* strongly favours the suggestion that the origin is the Old High German name *Madalhart*, meaning something like strong in discussion. A German dialect name for the gander is *gaeret* (for *Gerhard*, spear mighty), and in part of the Rhineland the jay is called *Markolf*, from Old High German *Markwolf*, lit. wolf of the marches. The same Teutonic name has given dialect French *marcou*,[2] defined by Cotgrave as

---

[1] The beast-epic obviously belongs to very primitive races. A fairly late example is the saga of *Cock Robin*. A still later one is the North American negro cycle of *Brer Rabbit*.

[2] Some authorities regard *marcou* and the synonymous *matou* as pet-forms of the names of the Evangelists.

' an old male cat, a gib [1] cat '.   In the Low German
version of *Reynard* (Reinke de Vos) the jay is
Marquart, Old High German *Markwart*, warden of
the marches.   It is as useless for the modern mind
to make conjectures as to the choice of these names
as it is to formulate theories for the origin of *Old
Nick*.

In some cases, however, it is possible to trace the
popular instinct for twisting an unfamiliar bird's
name into something more personal or for inter-
preting its cry in terms of human speech.   *Guillemot*,
a diving bird, is a French diminutive of *Guillaume*.
Our Elizabethan seamen sometimes call it *wilmot*
or *willock*, diminutives of *William*.   The oldest
recorded (c. 1600) Welsh name for the bird is
gwilym, i.e. William.   But, when we consider that
the Welsh word for gull is *gwlyan*, cognate with the
Breton *gwelan*, whence French *goéland*, we are
inclined to suspect that all the *William* names were
suggested by this ancient Celtic word.   *Willet*,
another diminutive of *William*, is the name of a
North American snipe, but this is due to its cry,
which sounds *pill-will-willet*.   At least, so they say !
It is curious that bird-cries do not sound alike to
different races, e.g. what to an English ear is *pewit*
is to a German *kiebitz*, while in Scotland it is *peese-
weep*.   Early ornithologists also assimilated the
sound to the name *Phoebe*, still used in America of a
kindred bird, generally called *peewee*.   The *kitti-
wake*, a kind of gull, also owes its name to its cry.

---

[1] *Gib* is for *Gilbert*.   *Gib-cat* is still used in dialect for the more
usual *tom-cat*.   *Gib* also means a male ferret and a male salmon.

The commonest of all our birds was long known as *Philip sparrow*. This dates, so far as records go,[1] from Skelton's lament, A Litel Boke of Phylip Sparowe, which belongs to the beginning of the 16th century. Both the full name and the shortened *phippe*, a sparrow, the latter occurring in Piers Plowman (1377), were probably suggested by the chirp. *Phip* (whence the surname *Phipps*) was one of the pet-forms of *Philip*. *Philippe* is also used for the bird in French dialect. *Old Francis* is a fenman's name for the heron. This is an elaboration of the earlier *frank*, ' apparently a rendering of the sound made by the bird ' (Oxford Dictionary). French *Louis*, the curlew (*courlis*), is obviously imitative of the cry. More elaborate is *bobolink*, an American bird whose call the early settlers interpreted as *Bob o' Lincoln*, just as another seemed to cry *whip-poor-will* and an arboreal insect to chirp *kitty-did* or *katy-did*. In such cases there is, however, always the possibility that some native name has been misunderstood or twisted into intelligibility ; but the Australian *laughing jackass* is genuine English.

It was at the beginning of the 16th century [1] that *parrot* began to replace the mysterious *popinjay*. As already mentioned, this is a diminutive of French

---

[1] i.e. dictionary records, for, as I have often shown, the study of surnames revolutionizes the chronology of the Oxford Dictionary. John Philipschanke, presumably nicknamed from his thin legs, was living in Yorkshire in 1379. So also William le Perot is found in the Writs of Parliament for 1277, i.e. more than two centuries before the first Oxford Dictionary record of *parrot*.

Pierre. There is, however, no trace of this sense in French, so the immediate source must be *Perrot*, a common medieval font-name, still surviving as a surname. *Parakeet* is a puzzle. French *perroquet* corresponds to Italian *parrochetto* and Spanish *periquito*. The Italian form is explained as a diminutive of *parroco*, a parson, which makes it a parallel to German *dompfaffe*, bullfinch, literally cathedral priest, and French *moineau*, sparrow, ' little monk '. The Spanish form is apparently a diminutive of *Perico*, pet-form of *Pedro*, i.e. Peter. Probably they are identical, but it is impossible to say which is the corrupted form. There is no doubt of the ornithological application of the very popular French name *Martin*.[1] The swift is in French *martinet*, perhaps in allusion to its flight southward about *Martinmas*, and the kingfisher is *martin-pêcheur*. Nor is there much doubt that the stormy *petrel* is connected with *St. Peter*, who attempted to walk on the water. Sailors call the bird *Mother Carey's chicken*, a name explained in a letter to the Sunday Times (April 10, 1932) as a corruption of the Latin *Mater Cara*, while the French sailors' name for it, according to the same authority, is *avis Sanctae Mariae*. One had no idea that early English and French shellbacks suffered so acutely from ' the paralysing effects of premature Latin '.

Madge howlet belongs to the same class as *magpie*, *jackdaw*, etc. The simple *Madge* is used in dialect

[1] The name was one of the commonest in France, and occurs in several proverbial phrases (see p. 131).

of both the barn-owl and the magpie. The latter
bird is also called in the south-west of England
Maggot, an old diminutive of *Margaret*.[1] Shakespeare has *maggot-pie* (Macbeth iii. 4) and Cotgrave
defines *jaquette* as ' a piannat or megatapie '. It is
impossible to say why some birds were given a
masculine name and others a feminine. In *poll
parrot*, as already noticed, the sexes are mixed, and
we shall see that the same is the case with the names
of the owl. The diminutive *owlet*, of comparatively
late appearance, is altered from the much older
howlet. As an *eaglet* is a little *eagle*, it seemed
natural to regard the (*h*)*owlet* as a little (*h*)*owl*,
which it is not, for *howlet* is used in Middle
English for the adult bird. It is borrowed from
French *hulotte*, ' madge-howlet ' (Cotgrave). This
is usually explained as derived from the Old High
German *ule* (now *eule*), an owl, with the aspirate
added by association with French *huer*, to hoot,
or howl (whence our *hue and cry*). Of course
the association between ' owls ' and ' howling ' is
very natural : cf. Latin *ulula*, owl, and *ululare*, to
screech.

The true explanation, in my opinion, is that
hulotte is the feminine of *Hulot*, an old diminutive of
the very common Old French font-name *Hue*, i.e.

---

[1] The common noun *maggot*, a metathesis of earlier *maddock*,
is no doubt due to the instinct for a personal name form. This
may have been helped by the fact that the magpie is the natural
enemy of the maggot. Thus Tusser, in his Lesson for Dairy-
maid Cisley—

If gentils be scrawling   (i.e. if maggots be crawling),
Call Maggot the pye.

Hugh. This name, shortened from *Hubert* (Old High German *Huguberaht*), was one of the favourites of the Middle Ages. In English it was commonly written *Hew* and *How*. Its diminutives have given the surnames *Hewett, Howitt, Hewlett, Hullett, Howlett, Hutchin, Houchin*, the first of which represents French *Huet*, of which the feminine form *huette* was also used in Old French for the screech-owl. Cotgrave gives the variant *huotte*, ' a howlet '. The *Hugh* origin of the bird-name is conclusively proved by the dialect variants of *howlet*, which include *hewlett* and *hullett*,[1] corresponding to the personal names given above. Moreover an obsolete name for the bird was *houchin* or *hob-houchin*, another diminutive of *Hugh*. A 17th-century translator of Boileau's Lutrin uses *hob-houchin* to render *hibou*, the general French name for the owl. Here, as in *hobgoblin, poll-parrot*, and *madge howlet*, the new familiar name was prefixed, when the *Hugh* origin of *houchin* was no longer realized. Another dialect name for the bird is *jenny hullett* (p. 120). We cannot tell why the redbreast should be *Robin* or the wren *Jenny* (also *Kitty*), but we can give a reasonable explanation of *Frank* for the heron and *Philip* for the sparrow. So, when it was a question of giving a familiar name to the nocturnal and generally invisible owl, what more natural than to choose one which punningly suggested the bird's chief characteristic ?

A sort of parallel to *madge howlet* and *hob-houchin*

[1] The English Dialect Dictionary gives nearly 30 variants, some obviously influenced by association with *owl*.

is *tomnoddy*. In the early 19th century this stood
for a young fool of fashion—

> My Lord Tomnoddy got up one day ;
> It was half after two,
> He had nothing to do,
> So his Lordship rang for his cabriolet.
>   (' Ingoldsby ', The Execution.)

A century earlier it was a nickname for the puffin,
known to the Scotch as *tammie norie*. *Tomnoddy*
is an elaboration of *noddy*, applied since the 16th
century to various sea-birds and also to a simpleton.
Noddy is a pet-form of Nicodemus, a name which,
we know not why, was used by the Middle Ages for
a fool. The bird was named from its supposed
stupidity,[1] and, when *noddy* ceased to express this
sufficiently, it was reinforced by the prefixed *Tom*,
which we find linked with *fool* as early as the 14th
century. The Durham Account Rolls for 1356–7
contain an entry of the funeral of *Thome fole*,
also referred to in the same record as *Thomas
fatuus*.

As far back as we can trace the history of words men
have been named from quadrupeds and quadrupeds
from men. In the case of words of obscure origin
it is sometimes difficult to decide which is the prior
sense. An example of this difficulty is the obsolete
talbot, a kind of hound. In the Chiswick High Road
there is still an inn called the Packhorse and Talbot.
The origin of the surname *Talbot* is unknown, but
this famous historic family dates back to the Con-

---

[1] Cf. *dodo*, which is Portuguese *doudo*, stupid, no doubt
ultimately related to our *dotterel*.

quest, its most illustrious member being John Talbot, Earl of Shrewsbury, ' Talbott oure goode dogge ' in a political rime of his day, who was killed at Castillon in 1453. The earliest mention of the hound is in Chaucer, who, however, treats it as a proper name (see p. 86), but it may, of course, be very much older. Tradition says that the family introduced the animal into England, but tradition usually lies. According to Dr. Johnson and the Oxford Dictionary, the hound appears in the family arms of the Talbots.

Another problematical example is *gibbon*, a most agile Indian ape brought to Europe by Dupleix in the 18th century. Buffon calls it an Indian word. Skeat suggests that this ' Indian ' word is probably the English *Gibbon*, a pet-form of *Gilbert*, of which the shortened *gib* was regular 14th century for a cat (see p. 122, n. 1). That *Gibbon* was applied to animals is shown by the fact that King John had a falcon so named. Here I have come across a bit of corroborative detail, viz. the ape's head which, in Rolvenden Church (Kent), surmounts the tombs of the *Gybbon* family, of much more ancient date than Buffon and Dupleix. The application of a personal name to an ape is almost inevitable. The intermediate stage appears in such a description as the Malay *orang-outang*, which a traveller of 1631 already interprets correctly as meaning ' homo silvae '.

One can hardly imagine a dog or a horse without a personal name. Legend has preserved the names of Actaeon's fifty hounds, who tore him to pieces, when, as a punishment for seeing Diana bathing, he was changed into a stag—

Like Sir Actaeon he, with Ringwood [1] at thy heels.
(Merry Wives, ii. 1.)

Argos, 'shimmering white', was the dog of Ulysses. Though old and forsaken, he recognized his master on his return from his wanderings. The still more mythical *Cerberus* has become synonymous with a forbidding doorkeeper. Apart from personal names of dogs we have the new class-names which come into existence, as new breeds of terriers are evolved to suit changing fashions, e.g. the *airedale*, from the valley of the *Aire* (Yorkshire), the *bedlington*, from a village in Northumberland, the *sealyham*, the name of a seat near Haverfordwest, and the *poltalloch*, first bred by Colonel Malcolm, of *Poltalloch* (Argyll). Probably older than any of these is the *clumber* (spaniel), from the Duke of Newcastle's seat (Notts).

The earliest horse that we know by name is probably *Pegasus*, the winged steed which sprang from the blood of Medusa slain by Perseus. The use of the name in connection with the poet's flights dates from Boiardo (15th century). More historical is Alexander's *Bucephalus* (bull-head), which is used allusively almost as often as Don Quixote's *Rosinante* (nag formerly !). Almost every medieval hero had

---

[1] A favourite name for a hound. Holyoak's Latin Dictionary (1612) gives a long list in which occur such names as *Babble, Blackfoot, Closebiter, Hillbred, Huntdoe, Killbuck, Lightfoot, Makespeed, Piedcoat, Quicksight, Rangehill, Shaghair, Scalecliff, Swiftfoot, Whirlwind, Whitetooth, etc.*

a famous charger, the most familiar perhaps being *Bayard* (see p. 117, n. 1).

The above examples are historical, literary or zoological, but, if we ransack early English and our expiring dialects, we find that there is hardly an animal which is not generically known by some familiar baptismal name. The same is true of other languages, e.g. Ménage, in his Origines de la Langue Françoise (1650), remarks that the ass is called *Martin*, the monkey *Robert*, the sheep *Robin*, the squirrel *Fouquet*,[1] the female goat *Guyonne*,[1] etc. In English dialect the ass is often called *Neddy* or *Dicky*, while in Scotland (and in many English counties) he is *Cuddy*, a fact which long made *Cuthbert* unpopular as a baptismal name. In various parts of France the ram is known as *Guérin*, *Martin*, *Michaud*, etc., and in German-Swiss he is *Benz*, a pet-form of *Bernhard*.

Restricting ourselves to English, we find that the fox is *Charley* and that the hare has been *Wat* (i.e. *Walter*) since the 15th century—

> By this, poor Wat, far off upon a hill,
> Stands on his hinder legs with listening ear,
> To hearken if his foes pursue him still.
> (Venus and Adonis.)

He is still called *Watty* by the poacher. In the Roman de Renard he is *Couard*, while in Middle English he was ironically called *Turpin*, from the valiant archbishop who fell at Roncevaux. Still

---

[1] *Fouquet* is a pet-form of one of the popular names in *Folk-*, people, and *Guyonne* is a feminine form of *Guyon*, diminutive of *Guy* (p. 2).

earlier (13th century) we find him as *Wimount*, from the Anglo-Saxon name *Wigmund*, meaning something like 'battle guardianship'. He shares with the cat the mysterious name *puss*, of which forms are found in most European languages and even in Afghan and Tamil. The same relationship appears in German, *Hinz* (p. 132) being applied both to the tomcat and the male hare; cf. *malkin* (p. 86).

The choice of such an unusual name as *Wigmund* is a mystery, but the use of *Martin* for an ass in French may be explained by the immense popularity of this baptismal name, a popularity connected especially with *St. Martin of Tours*.[1] In the Old French version of Reynard the Fox *Bernard* is the name of the ass. This may account for the fact that *Bernard* is ' a light brain'd or shittle-headed fellow ' (Cotgrave); or the depreciatory sense of the name may have led to its application to the animal. These two names, *Martin* and *Bernard*, rival *Jean* and *Pierre* in their allusive uses. We even have *parler d'autre Bernard* (or *Martin*) in the sense of changing the subject of conversation.

It is to the saga of *Reynard the Fox* that we owe a number of animal names which have a much wider European application than the examples hitherto mentioned. This famous collection of fox-stories, which Herder considered the greatest epic since Homer, is by far the most important monument we have of early folk literature or folk poetry. The best-known early versions are in Old French, but

---

[1] There are in France three or four hundred villages, townships, etc., called *Saint-Martin*.

the legends are found in all the European languages,
and most of the names are of Teutonic origin. Our
form *Reynard* represents the early Dutch or Flemish
spelling which Caxton adopted in his translation
from that language. The Low German version
Reinke de Vos had the honour of being turned into
modern German by Goethe in 1794. The Old
French for fox is *goupil*, registered by Cotgrave
(1611) as a ' vieux mot '. This comes from Vulgar
Latin *vulpeculus*, dim. of *vulpes*, fox. In the Old
French Roman de Renard (13th century) he is
Renard le goupil. He is also called *Renard le roux*,
with which name we may compare Chaucer's *Dan* [1]
Russell the fox (B. 4524). The complete replacement of the generic name by the personal name has
an approximate parallel in our *robin*. *Renard* is
Old High German *Reginhart*, strong in counsel. In
English the name was naturally confused with the
cognate and more familiar *Reginald*. Spenser calls
the fox *Reynold*, and even to-day the Sussex peasant
speaks of *Mister Reynolds* or *Mus' Reynolds*.

In the Low German version the ass is *Baldwin*,
valiant friend, a pet-form of which survives in
French *baudet*, jackass. *Isengrim*, iron helm, the
wolf, has not persisted, but the bear is in German
Braun, brown, and in English, via Dutch, *Bruin*.
More familiar in German is *Meister Petz*, but this
name, earlier *Bätz*, is simply a pet-form of *bär*, bear,
and has no connection with the epic. In the Low
German version the tom-cat is *Heinz* or *Hinz*, pet-
forms of *Heinrich*, Henry. In Old French he is

[1] Masculine form of *dame* ; cf. Spenser's *Dan Chaucer*.

Tibert, whence the allusion to *Tybalt's* nine lives in Romeo and Juliet (iii. 1) and the epithet 'rat-catcher' bestowed on him by Mercutio. The name is Old High German *Thiudberaht*, people bright.

One of the most familiar names from this source is of purely French origin. In Low German the cock is *Henning*, a pet-form of *Hans*, with a punning allusion to German *hahn*, cock, but this name is altogether eclipsed by *Chanticleer* (Old French *chantecler*, sing clearly). Chaucer tells the tale of Chauntecleer and Pertelote. The latter, *Partlet* in Shakespeare, is of unknown origin. In Old French the hen is also called *Pinte*, supposed to mean speckled [1]; cf. French *pintade*, guinea-fowl. Before we leave Reynard we may note that, besides the English *Charley* (p. 130), we find him adorned with such names as French *Bastien* (*Sebastian*), Spanish *Pedro*, and Swedish *Mickel* or *Mickel Räv*.[2]

The ape, probably a late addition to the epic, is called *Martin* in the Low German version (A.D. 1498), and his son's name is *Moneke*, which brings us to the vexed question of the etymology of *monkey*. Earlier than *Moneke* we find Old French *monequin*, evidently a diminutive of Flemish origin. Connected with these is obsolete Italian *monicchio*, explained by Florio (1598) as 'a pugge, a munkie, an ape'. The word *monkey* has not been found in English before 1530, and the early quotations suggest that the name was applied especially to pet monkeys,

[1] Vulgar Latin *pincta*, for *picta*, painted; cf. *pinto*, Spanish for a piebald, but, in Spanish America, a skewbald.
[2] *Räv* = fox,

marmosets. An older name was *jackanapes* (15th century), which, in spite of the popular association with *ape*, probably stands for ' Jack of Naples ', as Italy was the medieval source of supply for tame marmosets.[1] No doubt the Low German *Moneke* was brought to England by showmen. It is, like all the other Teutonic names in the Renard saga, of personal name origin. From the name-element *mun*, thought, etc., were formed a number of names of which the Low German diminutives were *Muncke*, *Mohnike*, *Möhnke*, etc., just as the pet-form of *Reginhart* was in Low German *Reinke* (p. 132). These still exist as surnames [2], and Heinrich Moneke and Johann Godeke [3] were envoys from Prussia to England in 1403. Moreover, I suggest that the choice of the name and its ready acceptance in England were partly due to popular association with *monk*, German *mönch*, Dutch and Low German *monik*. In my picture-book days I always associated the cowled *monk* with the *monkey*, and I find, on inquiry, that the childish experience of many potent, grave and reverend philologists was similar to my own.

If this etymology is, as I am convinced, correct, it offers one more example of the punning instinct which can sometimes be detected in this region of word-formation. The fact that the Breton peasant

[1] On the curious history of the word see my More Words Ancient and Modern.

[2] It is, of course, understood that, in all European languages, numbers of now rare or disused baptismal names survive as surnames. See, for example, *Jordan* and its derivatives (p. 60).

[3] A similar formation from one of the *God-* names (p. 80).

calls the pig by the illustrious Breton name *Rohan*
has no connection with any pig-breeding activities
of that noble house. It is simply the adoption of
a well-known name vaguely suggesting the dis-
tinctive ' note ' of the animal. As recently as the
World War *la famille Gautier* came into existence
as a collective name for the parasitic insects which
helped to make life in the trenches a misery for the
poilu. Here we have a punning formation from
the argotic *gau*, louse. *Turc*, the usual French
name for the larva of the cockchafer, destructive to
fruit-trees, may be of Celtic origin, but owes its
form and persistence to a hostile feeling which dates
back to the Crusades and to a belief thus expressed
by a writer of 1688—' Les poiriers de bon chrestien
(see p. 49) en sont sur tous endommagez, et c'est
pourquoi on a nommé ce ver Turc.' More accidental is the origin of *Norfolk Howard*, a humorous
euphemism for ' bug '. According to Mr. H. G.
Wells, in The Dream, ' Once upon a time, ran the
popular legend, a certain Mr. Bugg, seeking a less
entomological name, had changed his to Norfolk
Howard '. If Mr. Wells had consulted the Oxford
Dictionary (as even the most learned should do
before committing themselves in the matter of
words), he would have found that Joshua Bug's
announcement in the Times of June 26, 1862, has
nothing of the legendary, but is authentic and
documented history.

In addition to the use of simple names applied to
certain animals, our dialects are full of such compounds as *bubblyjock*, the turkey, where *jock* is the

Scottish form of *jack, jeffreycock*, the cockchafer, *natterjack*, a somewhat rare and particularly agile species of toad. The Oxford Dictionary describes this as of obscure formation. I should be inclined to see in the first element a perverted form (cf. *newt* for *ewt, nickname* for *ekename*) of the obsolete *atter*, poison, as in *attercop*, spider.

CHAPTER x

ON CALLING NAMES

THE meaning which we attach to the expression to 'call names' throws the usual light on human nature. Mrs. Wright [1] tells us that the English Dialect Dictionary registers ' approximately 1,350 words meaning to give a person a thrashing . . . 1,300 ways of telling a person he is a fool . . . and about 1,050 terms for a slattern '. Descriptions applicable to a kindly action, a wise man or a good housewife are not mentioned. Presumably they are a negligible quantity. Even terms which were originally complimentary soon acquire in popular psychology a satirical tinge. An example is *goodman*, once a title of dignity for the master of the house, and still so used in Scotland, but already in Shakespeare a contemptuous mode of address, like French *bonhomme*. The same fate has befallen the German *biedermann*, originally the type of plain, bluff honesty, but now a ' gaffer ', ' softy '. So the reader will find, possibly with regret, but certainly without surprise, that the words dealt with in this chapter are almost without exception uncomplimentary. [2]

[1] Rustic Speech and Folk-lore, Oxford, 1913.
[2] This applies also to our surnames of nickname origin. It is at least even betting that the original *Lillywhite* was swarthy,

The practice of giving what we may call label-names to fictional characters is strongly exemplified in the allegories and allegorical dramas of the Middle Ages. In the Romaunt of the Rose we find all the virtues and vices personified. Langland is a little more imaginative with his *Dowell*, *Dobet* and *Dobest*, the second (= do better) being described as 'Sire Doweles daughter' (Piers Plowman, B. ix. 12). The same psychology is responsible for the old saying that '*Brag* is a good dog, but *Holdfast* is a better'.

In the 16th century Rabelais called his amusing rascal *Panurge*, from Greek *panourgos*, lit. all-working, Jack of all trades, but defined by Liddell as 'ready for all crimes, unscrupulous, knavish, etc.' To Rabelais English owes *Gargantuan repast*, one suited to the giant *Gargantua*, and *Pantagruelism*, the kind of coarse bibulous humour with a serious purpose associated with his son *Pantagruel*. We find traces of the same tendency in Shakespeare, who uses the name *Parolles* for a wordy fool (All's Well That Ends Well), and ironically calls a witless tinker *Christopher Sly* (Taming of the Shrew). *Sly* originally meant acute, prudent, etc., and it is possible that *Christopher* may have implied stupidity, as its German pet-form *Stoffel* is synonymous with blockhead. When we get to the tawdry Restoration drama, this practice becomes almost

the original *Drinkwater* a toper, and the original *Wiseman* an ass. In the 18th century the name *Cunningham* was 'a punning appellation for a simple fellow' (Grose, Dictionary of the Vulgar Tongue, 1796).

exasperating. French comedy, its progenitor, indulged freely in stock names, e.g. *Géronte* (from
Greek *gerōn*, old man) for the derided father or
comic old husband ; but our own writers are so
helpful and exact in their descriptions that they
would seem to have composed their works for
morons. They suggest children addressing each
other as *Mr. Knowall* or *Miss Clever* or being reminded by their nurses not to forget *Mr. Manners.*
Opening Wycherley, we find among the dramatis
personae of his first play, Love in a Wood (1671),
Alderman Gripe, ' seemingly precise, but a covet-
ous, lecherous, old usurer of the City ' ; *Sir Simon
Addleplot*, ' a coxcomb, always in pursuit of women
of great fortunes ' ; *Mr. Dapperwit*, ' a brisk, con-
ceited, half-witted fellow of the Town ' ; *My Lady
Flippant*, ' Gripe's sister, an affected widow in dis-
tress for a husband, though still declaiming against
marriage ' ; *Mrs. Crossbite*, ' an old cheating jilt
(see p. 83) and bawd to her daughter '. This sort
of thing persisted till the end of the 18th century,
a particularly outrageous example being Macklin's
Sir Pertinax Macsycophant, and 19th-century Punch
still knew *Mr. Quiverful*, the impecunious father
of a large family, and *Sir Gorgius Midas*, the
millionaire sausage-maker. Two names of this type
have, however, met with general approbation, viz.
Lady Bountiful and *Boniface*, an innkeeper, both
from Farquhar's Beaux' Stratagem (1707). But
Farquhar's spelling is *Bonnyface.*

This trick was becoming unfashionable by the
middle of the 19th century, its last serious use

being perhaps in *The Fairchild Family*, the perpetration of which occupied Mrs. Sherwood between 1818 and 1847. Sterne called Smollett *Dr. Smelfungus* in allusion to his disgruntled account of his continental tour. Scott, with his dedications to *Dr. Dryasdust*, gave a word to the language, but his country schoolmaster, *Jedediah Cleishbotham* (from Scottish *cleish*, to whip), is not intelligible to the Southron. Then we have Thackeray's *Dr. Birch*, for a pedagogue, and *Lady Bareacres*, representing haughty impecuniosity. *Tadpole* and *Taper*, from Disraeli's *Coningsby*, have become types of the political schemer, and *Tadpoleonic* has been playfully used to describe a contemptible type of ambition. One regrets that Dickens should have been guilty of *Verisopht* (Nicholas Nickleby) and *Honeythunder* (Edwin Drood).

One of the earliest allusive uses of a surname preceded by a title is the recommendation of Sir John Harington [1] to trust to the three physicians, *Dr. Diet*, *Dr. Quiet* and *Dr. Merriman*. A modern witticism of the same type is the *Rev. Mr. Greenfields*, for a country-walk as a substitute for attendance at divine worship. With these compare the rustic *John* (or *Tom*) *Long the carrier*, for a slow or roundabout route, or the playful assumption of the name *John Blunt* by those who are rather proud of their bad manners. Fifty years ago cockneys would prelude their departure with the mystic words ' My name's *Walker* '.

[1] Author of Metamorphosis of Ajax (1596), an early work on sanitation.

The practice of punning on surnames is ancient. The most famous historic example occurs in Matthew xvi. 18. But such punning is usually unkindly and, especially in early youth, a cause of suffering to the victim (*experto crede* !). It is not a common practice to pun on one's own name, though the dying John of Gaunt makes great play with the adjective *gaunt* in a speech which provokes from the King the comment, ' Can sick men play so nicely with their names ? ' (Richard II., ii. 1). The more usual attitude is that of the bullying sea-captain in Charles Reade's Hard Cash, who, addressing Mr. Sharp, the mate, explains rather menacingly that his own name is *D——d Sharp*. It is to this elementary instinct that we must ascribe a whole series of appellations, partly taken from surnames which are susceptible of a punning interpretation, but more often arbitrarily constructed so as to have a surname appearance.

The Oxford Dictionary dates *simpleton*, described by Johnson as a ' low word ', from 1650 (it was probably much earlier in colloquial use). It describes the word as a ' fanciful formation ' and compares the dialect *idleton*, an idler. Skeat's explanation that it is formed with the French double diminutive *-et-on* is quite out of the question. Obviously it is a pseudo-surname suggested by the numerous English names derived from places ending in *-ton*. A more modern example is *singleton*, meaning a single card of any suit in a hand at whist, etc. According to Grose this well-established

surname [1] was also used in the 18th century with
very much the same meaning as *simpleton*. The
Oxford Dictionary and the English Dialect Dictionary give Scottish *pinkerton*, a person of small intelligence. *Pinkerton* is a village in Haddington-
shire. Its allusive use was perhaps suggested by
Scottish *pinkie*, small.

Bishop Corbet, who wrote Rewards and Fairies,
became in later life regrettably addicted, in the
company of his chaplain, to alcoholic excess, but,
as Mr. E. V. Lucas says, in Over Bemerton's, ' when
a chaplain is named *Lushington* . . . ! ' I fancy
that this term for one who loves the wassail-bowl
is archaic in England, though it is used several
times by ' Rolf Boldrewood ' in his tales of Australian life. In another Australian novel (Bail Up,
by Hume Nesbit) I find *swippington*, applied to
one too fond of indulging in *swipes*, a vulgarism
of the same type as *lush*. The surname *Lushington* is of old standing and has contributed eight
entries to the Dictionary of National Biography. A
convivial society, called the City of Lushington, met
at the Harp, Russell Street, till 1895, and claimed
to be 150 years old. The choice of the name was
probably due to *lush*, defined by Grose as ' strong
beer ', which is perhaps from the mysterious Shelta [2]
jargon. Hotten's Slang Dictionary (1864) quotes
from the Globe (Sept. 8, 1859) ' *Lush* and its derivatives claim *Lushington*, the brewer, as sponsor,' but

---

[1] From Singleton (Sussex or Lancashire). The surname is at
least as old as the 14th century.

[2] The cryptic slang of Gaelic tinkers.

this sort of statement does not carry much conviction. Of similar formation to the preceding words
is the rustic *skimmington*, a comic procession in
ridicule of an unhappy couple, but originally, as
shown by an illustration of 1639, a character im-
personating a wife beating her husband with a
skimmer. Finally, in The Rovers (in the Poetry
of the Anti-Jacobin), *Milord Beefington* is the name
of an Englishman resident on the Continent.

Less familiar are a similar collection of words in
-by, modelled on such familiar surnames as Busby,
Catesby, etc. Among those which are admitted to
the Oxford Dictionary are *rudesby*, used in Drant's
translation of Horace (1567) to render the *plebecula*,
or rabble ; *sneaksby*, equally ancient and found
both in Dryden and in Isaac Barrow's sermons ;
and *wigsby*, one wearing a wig, for which the earliest
authority is Grose. Of these *rudesby* is the best
recorded. It is used by Scott and later writers
affecting the archaic, and was even included in Ains-
worth's Latin Dictionary (1773), where it is glossed
' homo impudens, inverecundus, procax, protervus '.

Formations in *-ton* and *-by* are the commonest,
but there are a few other sporadic examples. The
Tudor and Stuart word *ingram*, ignorant, may be
a natural perversion, like *vagrom*, as in Dogberry's
charge to the watch—' You shall comprehend all
vagrom men ' (Much Ado, iii. 5) ; but it may
quite well be an assimilation to the common surname *Ingram*.[1] The Oxford Dictionary has copious

---

[1] Of Norman origin, its usual Old French form being Enguer-
rand. This corresponds to the rare Anglo-Saxon Ingelram.

records of *ingram* in the sense of *ignoramus*,[1] and it long survived in the north, though probably now obsolete. Apparently the Yorkshire *gawkshaw*, left-handed man, and the Somerset *gawkum*, simpleton, still flourish. They are formed from the dialect *gawk*, left-handed, clumsy, on the model of Yorkshire names in *-shaw*, wood (Bradshaw, Grimshaw, etc.) and west country names in *-combe*,[2] valley.

Less rural are *muggins* and *juggins*, both of which were surnames [3] for many centuries before they passed into slang. I frequently see the name *Juggins* on carts in Chiswick. *Muggins*, the older of the two, was perhaps chosen as allusive to *mug*, in the sense of simpleton, while *juggins* was a riming variation on the same theme. The great vogue of the latter was, I fancy, partly due to alliteration's artful aid, for the *Jubilee Juggins* was a young man who got rid of a large fortune in record time in the year of Queen Victoria's first jubilee (1887). Why *mugs* should be associated with stupidity is not clear, but it may be noted that French *cruche*, a jug or mug, also means a ' juggins '. *Mr. Hopkins*, ' a ludicrous address to a lame or limping man ' (Grose), is characteristic 18th-century wit, and the Cambridge *proggins* is an obvious ' surname ' perversion of *proctor*. The United States, with its

---

[1] The use of this 1st pers. plur. pres. indic. as a noun dates from a play with this title (1615) satirizing lawyers. It was originally a legal term (' we do not know ') used by a grand jury regarding evidence as inadequate.

[2] Cf. *bunkum*, for *Buncombe* (p. 101).

[3] *Muggins* is perhaps from *Maggie* (*Moggy*) and *Juggins* from *Jug* (p. 58).

strange mixture of surnames from every country in Europe, shows a more catholic spirit in such formations. Examples are *wisenheimer*, for a ' smart Aleck ', and *buttinsky*, for an intrusive personality.

One more example of the assimilation of a disparaging epithet to a surname form is *wiseacre*, properly a prophet or soothsayer, but commonly taken, as Blount (1656) says, ' in malam partem, for a fool '. It comes, via archaic Dutch, from German *weissager*, and its history is very complicated [1]; but its form is clearly due to such surnames as Goodacre, Greenacre, etc., in which *acre* = field, and especially Blackacre and Whitacre, once stock names for litigants. The *Widow Blackacre* of Wycherley's Plain Dealer, who is adapted from Racine's Comtesse in Les Plaideurs, is described as a ' petulant, litigious widow '. Much earlier stock names connected with the law courts are *John a' Nokes* and *John a' Stiles*, i.e. John at the oak and John at the stile, typical peasant names used (like A and B or X and Y) of the parties in a legal action. The Oxford Dictionary records them from the 16th century. Later are *John Doe* and *Richard Roe*, the fictitious plaintiff and defendant in the obsolete mixed action for ejectment. These names appear to have been selected in the same haphazard way as *Thomas Atkins* (p. 174).

In the figurative use of the surnames, real or artificial, already mentioned the punning intention is generally on the surface, but there are earlier

[1] See my More Words Ancient and Modern, pp. 185–7.

examples of which the interpretation remains obscure. John Skelton, who died in 1529, uses two
names allusively—

> This pevysch proud, thys prendergest,
> When he is well, yet can he not rest.
>> (Skelton, Laureate, 6.)

> It was a bullyfant,
> A greedy cormorant.
>> (Elynour Rummyng, 520.)

Prendergast comes from a hamlet in Pembrokeshire
and *Bullivant* is a corruption of the Franco-English
Bonenfant (Good-child), but Skelton's selection of
these names as types of ambition and greed is as
mysterious as his contemporary Udall's use of *Lil-
burne*, a surname which, in spite of its English
appearance, is no doubt from *Lillebonne* [1] (Seine-
Inférieure). Apparently it means, like the words
with which it is coupled, something like clown or
bumpkin—

> Ye are such a calfe, such an asse, such a blocke,
> Such a lilburne, such a hoball, such a lobcocke.
>> (Ralph Roister Doister, iii. 3.)

Udall is also our earliest authority for *Philip* and
Cheyney, which the 16th century used, rather oddly,
for *Tom*, *Dick* and *Harry*. I say oddly, because,
as a rule, only pet-forms of very familiar Christian
names are used in this way, while here we have
the formal *Philip* linked with the rather aristo-
cratic surname *Cheyney*, which is derived from one

---

[1] Such Anglicization of surnames of French origin is not
uncommon ; cf. *Falconbridge* from *Fauquembergue* (Pas de
Calais).

of the many French places called *Chênay* or *Chesnay*
(oak grove). Tusser accounts for his early failures
in agriculture by the fact that—

> Loiterers I kept so meany (many),
> Both Philip, Hob and Cheany.

A worsted material called *cheyney* [1] was also playfully elaborated into *Philip and Cheyney*, a good
example of the curiously illogical and pointless
nature of this type of ' humour '.

One of the earliest examples I have found of a
surname used in this inexplicable way is *Sibree*,[2]
applied by Caiaphas to Christ in the Towneley
Mysteries (c. 1460). The name is not uncommon
in the Wakefield region, to which these plays belong,
but history does not tell us what bearer of the name
had given it an evil reputation in the West Riding.
One more possible instance is *Casbald*, applied as
a term of reproach to Mary Magdalene both in the
Towneley Mysteries and the somewhat earlier York
Mysteries—

> Go home, casbalde with thi clowte,

which seems to be identical with the surname *Case-
bolt* or *Cashbolt*, of (to me) unknown origin. Probably the latest coinage of this type is *hooligan*,
which, though too recent to be found in the Oxford
Dictionary, was long ago adopted in Russia. The
original *Hooligans* were a family of Irish origin who

[1] Named from *China*, which was pronounced *Cheyney* by
educated people well into the 19th century.

[2] It represents Anglo-Saxon *Sigebeorht* (victory bright), which
normally becomes *Seabright*. For the form *Sibree* cf. *Kircud-
bright*, i.e. the Church of Cuthbert, pronounced *Kirkoobree*.

enlivened the Surrey side about the end of the 19th century.[1] The much earlier *hoodlum*, appearing in San Francisco about 1870, has been ' explained ' as an unsuccessful anagram of the Irish name *Muldoon* (!), but its true origin remains as mysterious as that of the synonymous Australian *larrikin*.

Earlier even than *Sibree* is *Jaudewin*, a 14th-century term of reproach. This is an Anglo-French name corresponding to the Anglo-Saxon *Goldwine* (the same man is called indifferently *Jeudewin* and *Goldewin* in the Close Rolls for 1204–27) and survives in the surname *Jeudwin* (cf. *Jawdewin's Lane*, Oxford) ; but, in its figurative application, it was perhaps rather a baptismal name than a surname. Cf. *Gerard*, applied in the Cursor Mundi (13th century) to Goliath, Herod, and Antichrist, and, in the 14th century, to the Devil.

The popular tendency to make anything look like a surname even appears in place-name nomenclature. *Jervaulx*, in the North Riding, is locally *Jarvis* ; *Selmeston*, near Lewes, is *Simpson* ; and there is even a Norfolk village called *Thompson*, for earlier *Tumeston*, probably the ' town ' of a Scandinavian named Tumma.

As we have seen, names in *-ton* preponderate in artificial surnames used with a satirical implication. Along with these goes the adjectival formation *grumbletonian*, from an imaginary *Grumbleton*. This name was applied, at the end of the 17th cen-

---

[1] I had this information from a house-surgeon at Guy's who spent some time in patching up the results of *Hooligan* activity.

tury, by the ' Court party ' to the ' Country party '.
It was modelled on *grindletonian*, the name of a
' familist ' sect which sprang up in Yorkshire early
in the same century, presumably at the village of
Grindleton in the West Riding. The *muggletonians*
took their name from a fanatic named *Lodowicke
Muggleton*, who, in 1651, claimed to be one of the
' witnesses ' of Revelation xi. 3–6. *Gothamite*, for
an imbecile, is an allusion to the ' wise men of
Gotham ', the place being usually identified with
Gotham, Notts. The *fools of Gotham* are mentioned
in the Towneley Mysteries.[1] In German they are
the *Schildbürger*, perhaps originally burgesses carrying shields,[2] but popularly associated with *Schildau
bei Torgau*, and the same lack of intelligence was
attributed by the Greeks to the *Abderites*, the inhabitants of *Abdera*[3] in Thrace. A *smart Aleck* is
sometimes called in German a *Schlauberger*, as
though from an imaginary *Schlauberg* (*schlau* = sly),
or a *Schlaumeyer*, in imitation of the hundreds of
German surnames ending in *-meyer, -meier*, farmer.
Cf. *biedermeyer* (see p. 137), used as a name for a
characteristic German style of furniture and decora-
tion. During the World War the evader of military service (French *embusqué*, English ' *Cuthbert* ')
was called in Germany *Drückeberger*, from *sich*

[1] See p. 147.

[2] Cf. *spiessbürger*, a ' philistine ', lit. burgess armed with a pike.

[3] Birthplace of Democritus, the ' laughing philosopher ', who
is sometimes called the *Abderite*, just as Aristotle is called the
Stagirite, from *Stagira* (Macedonia), Virgil the *Mantuan*, Livy
the *Patavinian*, from *Padua*. The epithet *Theban swan*, for
Pindar, may have suggested Ben Jonson's *swan of Avon* for
Shakespeare.

drücken, to vamose, decamp, shirk.   Flügel-Schmidt-
Tanger's Dictionary (1896) has *Da drücke ich mich*,
' my name is Walker, Hookey Walker '.

This brings us to a new group of witticisms, if
such they can be called, which start from puns on
place-names.   Our old collectors of rustic and proverbial sayings (Fuller, Ray, Grose, etc.) have
copious records of these allusions, sometimes quite
unintelligible, e.g. ' As sure as God's in Gloucester-
shire ',[1] ' The constable of Openshaw (near Manchester) sets beggars in stocks in Manchester ' ;
sometimes expressing a sort of parochial malevo-
lence, e.g. ' When Ex'ter was a furzy down, Kirton
(Crediton, Devon) was a mayor-town,' or the 16th-
century prayer ' From *hell*, *Hull* and *Halifax*, Good
Lord deliver us '.   The last is thus explained by
Ray—

> This is a part of the beggers and vagrants Litany.   Of these
> three frightful things unto them it is to be feared that they
> least fear the first, conceiving it the farthest from them.   Hull
> is terrible to them as a town of good government, where beggers
> meet with punitive charity, and it is to be feared are oftener
> corrected than amended.   Halifax is formidable for the law
> thereof, whereby theives taken in the very act of stealing cloth
> are instantly beheaded with an engine without any further legal
> proceedings.   Doubtless the coincidence of the initial letters of
> these three words help'd much the setting on foot this proverb.

The fullest record of this kind of ' literature '
will be found in Mr. Apperson's learned compilation, English Proverbs and Proverbial Phrases (London, 1929).   In some of the sayings the punning

---

[1] Traditionally, from the great number of religious foundations
in that county.   Cf. the German *Gott in Frankreich*, as a symbol
for being ' in clover '.

intention is obvious. The insubordinate are told
that they will be sent to *Birchin Lane* (in the City),
the reckless are warned that they will come home
by *Weeping Cross* (a hamlet in Staffordshire) or
that they are on the way to *Needham* (villages in
Norfolk and Suffolk). According to Fuller, ' They
are said to be on the high way to Needham which
hasten to poverty.' The stupid are said to be
' born at *Little Witham* '.[1] A triple pun is contained in the aphorism, recorded by Fuller, that
' He that fetcheth a wife from *Shrewsbury* must
carry her into *Staffordshire*[2] or else shall live in
Cumberland'. In German a *Nassauer*, lit. man from
Nassau, is a sponger, bilker. This is a pun on *nass*,
wet, which in German thieves' slang means penni-
less. With to *go to Bedfordshire*, i.e. to bed, cf.
the corresponding German *nach Bethlehem gehen*.
Swift couples this with a synonymous allusion to
the *land of Nod* (Genesis iv. 16). Toby, M.P., who
used to contribute ' Essence of Parliament ' to
Punch, was described as *member for Barks* (i.e.
Berkshire). More restricted localities are referred
to in *Queer Street*, not recorded before the 19th
century, for which modern American has coined
the contrasted *Easy Street* ; the *Marylebone* (i.e.
marrowbone) *stage*, equivalent to *Shanks's mare* or
pony ; and *Liberty Hall*, modelled on the obsolete
Cutpurse Hall and *Ruffians' Hall*, names for resorts
of criminals. The later *Bachelors' Hall* is first
recorded in Dickens.

---

[1] *Witham* (' white home ') is a common place-name.
[2] Cf. *Stafford law* (see p. 103).

We may compare with these products of popular
fancy a few imaginary regions named by men of
genius. The oldest are the *Atlantis* of Plato and
the *Nephelococcygia*, Cloud-Cuckoo-land, coined by
Aristophanes for the city of the birds. The *land
of Cockaigne*, an ideal happy land of ease and
plenty, is from French *Cocagne* (12th century). It
has been conjecturally derived from German *kuchen*,
cake.[1] Of later date is the corresponding German
Schlaraffenland, lazy-ape (?) land, for which 16th-
century English used *lubberland*. The most famous
of all such formations is More's *Utopia* (1516),
which has become European, and of which Samuel
Butler's *Erewhon* (1872) is a very unimaginative
variant. *Eldorado*, the imaginary golden city, is
first mentioned in English in Raleigh's Discoverie
of Guiana (1596). *Golconda*, supposed to blaze with
diamonds, is an old name for Hyderabad. Swift's
Lilliput, *Brobdingnag* and *Laputa* (the *Isle of
Laputa* is a caricature of the Royal Society) seem
to have been quite arbitrarily formed. The adjectives derived from all these are still in use, especially
lilliputian. With the Scottish *Kennaquhair*, know-
not-where, cf. the synonymous German *Weissnichtwo*.
Anthony Hope's *Ruritania* (Prisoner of Zenda) has no
apparent meaning, but may be mentioned here, as
the adjective *Ruritanian* is now a recognized description of romances dealing with imaginary Balkanoid
principalities of homicidal atmosphere.

The most familiar and, at the same time, most

---

[1] *Land o' cakes*, a name given to Scotland since the 17th
century, does not refer to luxury, but to oatmeal cake.

mysterious phrase of all, if it really belongs to this group, is to *send to Coventry*, which is recorded from the middle of the 18th century, but was no doubt in colloquial use much earlier. As many far-fetched explanations have been given, I venture to put forward another. The word *convent* was formerly *covent*, as still in *Covent Garden*, and was applied to a religious house for either sex. It does not seem impossible that *sending to Coventry* may have been a clumsy pun of the *go to Bedfordshire* (p. 151) type, implying the relegation of the culprit to a place of silence and seclusion. I put forward this theory with trepidant modesty.

Word-plays of the kind illustrated in this chapter generally belong to a rudimentary type of psychology. They are easily paralleled in other European languages, e.g. *My name's Walker* (p. 140) may be compared with the synonymous Spanish *llamarse* (to be called) *Andana*, from *andar*, to go. I have even heard *Popoffsky* used in the same way (cf. *Buttinsky*, p. 145). Although they are seldom admitted even to our most comprehensive dictionaries, they can be discovered in plenty by the searcher of medieval literature, early examples being often distinguished by a crudity that makes quotation difficult.[1]

[1] For an admirable essay on this feature of Old French literature see Tobler's Verblümter Ausdruck und Wortspiel in altfranzösischer Rede (Vermischte Beiträge, zweite Reihe, Leipzig, 1906).

CHAPTER XI

XENOPHOBIA

THERE is a tradition that the passing of an inoffensive stranger through a Black Country village used to inspire some such dialogue as—' Oo's that? '—' Dunno '—' 'Eave 'arf a brick at 'im.' A philological examination of terms descriptive of the foreigner, his language, and his supposed habits would tend to show that this attitude is proper to mankind as a whole, and that, in all ages and regions, the Jews have no dealings with the Samaritans.[1] The language of the foreigner is an obvious absurdity. We know that to the Greeks all other races were *bar-bar-ians*, and that the corrupted Attic spoken by the Athenian colonists of *Soloi*, in Cilicia, was branded as *solecism*. It is dramatic justice that *Greek* itself should have become, since Shakespeare's time (Julius Caesar, i. 2), synonymous with the unintelligible. *Hebrew* has occasionally been used in the same way. *St. Giles's*[2] *Greek*, *pedlars' French*, and *thieves' Latin*[3] are descriptions

[1] Mr. Mencken, in his American Language (p. 353), gives twenty-three more or less opprobrious epithets bestowed on immigrants by the native-born, nearly all of which are quite unfamiliar to the Englishman.

[2] From a low quarter of London.

[3] As this is recorded only in Scott, it may be one of his inventions.

of rogues' slang. It is also to be noted with regret
that French *Grec* is used for a cardsharper; but the
finer side of the national character is reflected in
the usually misquoted—

> When Greeks join'd Greeks, then was the tug of war.
> (Lee, Rival Queens, iv. 2.)

Latin has, on the whole, fared better, though we
find such disparaging compounds as *dog-Latin* and
kitchen-Latin. Italian *latino* means not only *Latin*,
but also clear, intelligible, and it is used as a noun
for learning, doctrine. The Gaelic derivatives of
the word have somewhat similar senses. In Old
French *latin* had almost the meaning of language,
especially as used for argument or persuasion;
hence the expressions 'Être au bout de son latin'
and 'Perdre son latin'. It was also commonly
used by the Old French poets to describe the 'sweet
jargoning' of birds—

> Cil oisel chascun matin
> S'estudient en leur latin
> A l'aube du jour saluer.
> (Roman de la Rose.)

The habit of attributing perfidious instincts to
the ancestral enemy is reflected in the Latin *Punica
fides*, used by Sallust for treachery. With this we
may compare our own 18th-century *French faith*
and the similar use of *Spanish* in the 16th century.
Compounds and phrases containing the word *French*
are almost innumerable. They are also, except in
literal descriptions of national products, largely
uncomplimentary, John Bull always feeling an

inherited distrust for all that is *Frenchified*. This appears in the deterioration in sense of *French leave*, applied in the 18th century to the French practice of leaving a social gathering without bothering one's hostess with a formal leave-taking. The French equivalent is *filer à l'anglaise* !

Almost equally familiar is *Dutch*. It is noteworthy that *Frenchman* and *Dutchman* are the only compounds of the Englishman, Welshman type applied by us to foreigners.[1] In the Middle Ages, and well into the 17th-century, *Dutch* (*High* or *Low*) was a comprehensive term for the language and inhabitants of all Teutonic countries, even including Scandinavia. From about the year 1600 it begins to have special reference to Holland, and it is this meaning which is reflected in most of our ' *Dutch* ' colloquialisms, e.g. *double Dutch* for gibberish, or ' If (such is the case, etc.), I'm a *Dutchman* '. Most of the opprobrious allusions connected with the word spring from 17th-century rivalry and warfare, e.g. *Dutch courage*, valour inspired by drink, of which Waller wrote as early as 1665—

> The Dutch their wine and all their brandy lose,
> Disarmed of that by which their courage grows.

It is strange that the legend of the *Flying Dutchman*, or phantom ship, which must be old among seamen, is not found in print earlier than Scott's note to Rokeby (ii. 11), where it is described as ' a well-known nautical superstition '. It is difficult to say

---

[1] The man of *Turcoman*, *Musulman*, is quite unrelated, though Dryden uses *Musulwoman* (this is like *viqueen* from *vik-ing*).

why a *Dutch uncle* should be a monitor of unusual severity. Perhaps the sense has been influenced by Dutch *baas*, uncle, whence our *boss*, the *patruae linguae verbera* of Horace having a distinct flavour of the ' bossy '.

A curious survival is the military *old sweat*, for a veteran soldier. Although this has no dictionary history, I have little doubt that it is the German *alter Schwede*, lit. old Swede, similarly used during the Thirty Years War and brought back by Dugald Dalgetty and his comrades. The most striking example of the conversion of a racial name into a common noun is of course *slave*. This is found in some form in most European languages, from the 9th century onward, after the reduction of some *Slavonic* population of Central Europe to a servile condition. A parallel is the Anglo-Saxon *wealh*, foreigner, also Briton (*Welshman*), slave ; and the most probable etymology of *coolie* is from the tribal name of a degraded Indian race.

Reverting for a moment to the British Isles, we find, besides such simple juxtapositions as *Scotch collops*, *Irish stew*, and *Welsh rabbit*,[1] certain xenophobic applications of our racial names. *False as a Scot* is registered, with regret, by Ray in the 17th century, and *Scot* is also archaic slang for that form of sudden anger which, with a dig at a kindred nationality, is called a *paddy*. The race-course practice of *welshing* is a slur on another Celtic branch, and readers of the author's age will remember a time when ' Go on ! You're *Irish* ' was a familiar

[1] *Welsh rarebit* is an etymologizing absurdity.

taunt with the less cultured cockney. Various pestilent thorny growths in New Zealand are known as *Scotchman*, *Irishman* and *Spaniard*. It need hardly be said that the Sassenach has received similar treatment from the dreamy Celt. The stolid complacency with which we regard our own national virtues found expression, as early as the 17th century, in the adjective *un-English*, the first Oxford Dictionary quotation for which is from the Histriomastix (1633) of that grim Puritan William Prynne—' So unmanly, degenerous, and un-English (if I may so speake) in all their conversation.'

Many nations are personified, by themselves and others, in some individual of marked characteristics. *John Bull* first appears in Arbuthnot's satire (1712), in which France is represented by the uncomplimentary *Lewis Baboon*. *Jacques Bonhomme* and *der deutsche Michel* have long been representative of the great peasant populations of France and Germany. From the former comes *Jacquerie*, the French peasant revolt of the 14th century. *Uncle Sam* has stood for the United States since the beginning of the 19th century. There is little doubt that it is a facetious interpretation of the letters *U.S.*, though attempts have been made by etymologists to drag in this or that individual Samuel. On the other hand, it is believed that *Brother Jonathan*, about equivalent to *Uncle Sam*, really owes his existence to Washington's way of addressing *Jonathan Trumbull*, governor of Connecticut.

At the time of the Crimean War, the battle of

Inkerman (Nov. 5, 1854) was celebrated by a patriotic rhymester with—

> You'll please to remember the Fifth of November,
> Sebastopol powder and shot,
> When General Liprandi met John, Pat and Sandy,
> And a jolly good licking he got.

Pat and *Paddy*, from the patron saint of Ireland, and *Sandy*, from the common Scottish name *Alexander*, do not seem to be older than the 18th century. The United States prefers *Mick* for the Irishman. Up to the end of the 18th century an Irishman was commonly called *Teague*, from the Irish name *Tadhg*, ' fancifully identified with Thaddeus' (Oxford Dictionary). It occurs in Lillibullero, the famous song against James II.'s Irish troops, which was said to have sung the King out of his kingdom, and which soothed Uncle Toby—

> Ho! broder Teague, dost hear de decree?
> Lilli Burlero, bullen-a-da,
> Dat we shall have a new deputie. . . .

Much older than *Sandy* is the variant *Sawney*. On April 9, 1667, Pepys saw a play entitled Sawney the Scot. The later development of the sense of simpleton is inexplicable, especially to Scots. *Taffy*, i.e. *David*, is recorded as a Welshman since c. 1700.

During the War, *Sammy* (from *Uncle Sam*) was sometimes used for an American soldier, as *Tony* (*Antonio*) was for a Portuguese, while the enemy was known as *Fritz*, a pet-form of *Friedrich*, or *Jerry* (p. 21), the American troops rather favouring *Heine*, from *Heinrich*. *Boche*, which is not a proper name, long ante-dates the War. *Alboche* is given

as a name for a German in Villatte's *Parisismen*
(a dictionary of French slang) of 1890. It is an
argotic perversion of *Allemand*, perhaps suggested
by the slang *tête de boche*, blockhead, registered in
the same compilation and often applied at a much
earlier date to a ' square-headed ' German. A name
connected with an older war is *pandy*, given to
the rebel sepoys in the Indian Mutiny. *Pande* was
a common surname among high-caste sepoys of the
Bengal army, and one of the name, a soldier of the
34th regiment, started a mutiny by killing a British
officer at Barrackpur (March 29, 1857). For *dago*,
an American term for a Southern European of Latin
race, see p. 1. The Oxford Dictionary dates it
only from 1888, but the Elizabethans anticipated
the name, for Dekker, writing in 1613, calls a
Spaniard a *Diego*. To the Mexican the Englishman
or United States American is a *gringo*. This
Spanish word is perhaps a corruption of *griego*,
Greek, used in the sense of unintelligible gibberish
(cf. p. 154). Mr. Bernard Shaw is said to have
elicited roars of laughter from an American audience
with the line (in The Applecart) that ' an American
is a wop pretending to be a Pilgrim Father '. The
origin of *wop*, an Italian, remains to be discovered.
Equally mysterious is the process by which *Chinaman* has become *Chink* in the United States.

Of all familiar or humorous national nicknames
none has excited so much etymological conjecture
as *Yankee*. Since 1765, and probably from a much
earlier date, it has been a nickname for a New
Englander, or, more widely, an inhabitant of the

Northern States. In the latter sense it was especially used by the Southerners during the War of Secession (1861–5). In English it has always been a general name for an American of the United States. Leaving out fantastic derivations of the ' anecdotic ' type, the favourite etymology for a long time was a back-formation (cf. *Chinee*) from *Yengeese*, supposed to be an Indian corruption of *English* and made familiar by the novels of Fenimore Cooper. A much more probable origin is the Dutch *Janke*, a diminutive of *Jan*, John, which may have been at first applied to the Dutch inhabitants of the New England states. This receives support from the fact that a competent North American pirate known as *Captain Yankey* or *Yanky Duch* is frequently mentioned in official records of the 17th century. If this is correct, and I see no reason to doubt it, *Yankee* belongs ultimately to the same category as *Pat, Taffy, Tony*, etc.

Two names of Eastern races have had a curious destiny in English. It was the great Lord Shaftesbury who first described the neglected urchins of London as ' City *Arabs*, like tribes of lawless freebooters '. French sometimes calls the type *Gavroche*, the name of a typical street-arab in Victor Hugo's Les Misérables. *Turk* was applied in crusading times to all Mohammedans and unbelievers (cf. ' Jews, Turks, infidels and heretics ', in the Good Friday Collect), and was also taken as a type of brutality and cruelty. *Young Turk* is, I suppose, still used of a naughty boy. It was Carlyle, who, in 1876, wrote impolitely of the *unspeakable Turk*.

Almost equally vague was *Saracen*, originally ' among the later Greeks and Romans, a name for the nomadic peoples of the Syro-Arabian desert, who harassed the Syrian confines of the Empire ' (Oxford Dictionary). The Middle Ages connected the *Saracens* with *Sarah*, the wife of Abraham. The true origin of the name, which was later applied to all the Moslem adversaries of the crusaders, is very uncertain. A wooden *Saracen*, or ' Turk's head ', was used as a figure to be tilted at, and the *Saracen's head* passed from heraldry to the sign-boards of many famous old inns. The popular form was *Sarsen*, still used of scattered sandstone boulders, *Sarsen stones*, in Wiltshire, and from the same word was probably formed *sarsenet* or *sarcenet*, an archaic name for a fine silk cloth. This suggests *tartan*, originally a rich fabric imported from China via *Tartary*,[1] and the *Tartars* themselves. Properly they are *Tatars*, but their hordes made such an unfavourable impression on Eastern Europe that they were promptly connected with the Latin *Tartarus*, hell. The first English record of the name is in Chaucer, in the Squire's unfinished story of Cambuscan [2] (i.e. Jenghiz Khan). The transferred sense of an awkward customer or a termagant has given the phrase to *catch a Tartar*, which is found in

[1] Among other memories of the ancient trade routes between Asia and Europe are *buckram*, probably from *Bokhara*, and *organdie*, from *Urjend*, in Turkestan, once a mart for Chinese silks traded to Persia by the Parthians.

[2] Or call up him that left half-told
The story of Cambuscan bold.

(Penseroso.)

the 17th century.   Grose gives one of those ' anecdotic ' explanations dear to the early word-hunter—

> This saying originated from a story of an Irish soldier in the
> Imperial service, who, in a battle against the Turks, called out
> to a comrade that he had caught a Tartar.   ' Bring him along,
> then,' said he.   ' He won't come,' answered Paddy.   ' Then
> come along yourself,' replied his comrade.   ' Arrah ', cried he,
> ' but he won't let me.'

It is natural that the name of such fierce invaders
as the *Tartars* should acquire a xenophobic sense.
Vandal, a wilful destroyer of the artistic and venerable, alludes to the sacking of Rome in 455 by
Genseric, King of the *Vandals*, a Germanic tribe.
Alaric, King of the *Goths*, had done the same in
410.   *Gothic* was at one time opposed to *classic*, as in
Gothic architecture, which had a suggestion of the
barbarous before the Romantics of the 18th century
made the old Teutonic word fashionable.   Our early
philologists used *Gothic* as a vague term for Teutonic.
It was in the 5th century that Attila and his *Huns*
overran a great part of Europe, but the figurative
sense of ' a reckless or wilful destroyer of the beauties
of nature or art ; an uncultured devastator ' (Oxford
Dictionary), is comparatively modern.   The use of
Hun for German, found many years before the War,
dates from a speech made by the ex-Kaiser in 1900
to his troops starting for China.   The *Parthians*,
an equestrian tribe of western Asia, were famous
for their skill in shooting backwards ; hence *Parthian
shot*, for a lady's ' last word ' before her exit—

> Or like the Parthian I shall flying fight.
> (Cymbeline, i. 7.)

Philistine, an uncultured and uninteresting bour-
geois, comes from Germany university slang.
Carlyle and Matthew Arnold share the responsi-
bility of having introduced it into English.

The hereditary enmity of two European races is
reflected in the French *querelle d'Allemand,* which
Cotgrave defines as ' an idle slight, or drunken con-
tention ; a frivolous or vain altercation ', and the
attitude of one province to another in *réponse de
Normand,* an evasive answer. *Gasconnade,* boastful
talk, reflects the character attributed by the French
to the inhabitants of one of the southern provinces.
Provincial hostility appears also in *Schwabe,* lit.
Swabian, the usual German name for the cockroach.
Our own folklore is full of sayings which suggest
that the people of the next county or town are not
much good, e.g. in Lancashire to *come Yorkshire
over* a man is to trick him in a bargain. The
Athenians regarded the *Boeotians* as hopelessly
stupid. Still worse was the reputation of the *Helots,*
the inhabitants of Helos,[1] reduced to a servile condition by the Spartans, and, according to Plutarch's
story, made to serve as awful examples (' drunken
helots ') to their masters' children. Xenophobic in
origin are the architectural supports called *caryatides,*
representing the women of *Caryae,* and emblematical
of the abject slavery to which they were reduced
as a punishment for Caryae having joined the
Persians. *Sybarite,* from the Greek city of *Sybaris*
in southern Italy, has always been contemptuous.

---

[1] This traditional origin of *Helot* is now regarded as ' popular
etymology '.

Corinthian and *Ephesian* both had the sense of debauchee, softened in Shakespeare to that of boon companion, 'lad of mettle' (1 Henry IV., ii. 4). It was about the year 1800 that a *Corinthian* became definitely a 'swell' of sporting tastes.

More pleasing qualities are associated with *Arcadia*, the home of the rural god *Pan* and of the ideal pastoral life. By popular association with the Greek *pan*, neuter of *pas*, all, *Pan* later became the personification of nature, whence *panic* (terror), inspired by the mysterious night sounds of hill and vale. *Attic*, or Athenian, has always connoted the civilized and urbane, and for the Romans *Attic salt* (*sal Atticus*) was synonymous with polished wit. The architectural *attic* has the same etymology. *Sparta* has a creditable record for stoicism and simplicity, and its alternative name *Laconia* has supplied us with an epithet for speech which is brief and to the point.

Greeks and *Trojans* have been inseparable in history. The Elizabethans used *Trojan* very much in the sense of *Corinthian*, generally linking it alliteratively with the adjective *true*. The Oxford Dictionary finds no example of *like a Trojan* before the 19th century, though its sense is implied in a Middle English quotation from Trevisa (1387).

There are a good many traces in language of Christian brutality towards the Jew. The phrase *worth a Jew's eye* (Merchant of Venice, ii. 5), i.e. of great value, would seem to be suggested by Front-de-Boeuf's methods. In the Middle Ages all sorts of midnight iniquities and unholy rites were attributed to the Jews, with the result that the word *sabbat* acquired in French the sense of a sorcerers' nocturnal gathering, pandemonium. This may possibly account for the *Jew's harp*, earlier also *Jew's trump*, which, according to Miss Murray's Witchcraft in Western Europe, was a favourite instrument at the ' witches' sabbath '. In one case at least the *Jew* was confused with *Judas*. *Judas-tree* [1] is the popular name for the elder, on which the traitor is supposed to have hanged himself. An ear-shaped fungus which grows commonly on the same tree is the *auricula Judae*, incorrectly rendered into English by *Jew's ear*. *Judas* is used in both English and French for a small grating through which one can watch without being seen. One of the latest examples of racial bad manners is the nickname *yid* for a Jew, a back-formation from *yiddish* (German *jüdisch*), the *lingua franca* of the Israelites, made up from various sources but written in the Hebrew character.

[1] In French erroneously *arbre de Judée* (Judaea).

CHAPTER XII

OUR LUNATIC CONTRIBUTOR

A S will be gathered by anyone who has had the patience to get through this book, I incline to the opinion that the part played by proper names in the creation of our vocabulary has been underestimated in the past, and I endeavour to prove (so far as one can use the word ' prove ' in matters etymological) that many words for which no origin has been found by the Oxford Dictionary are petrified personal names. Quite apart from all influences of geography, history, myth, literature, and the individual discoverer, inventor, etc., we have to do with that odd human bent for personification and anthropomorphism which is especially characteristic of childhood and of the primitive type of mind. In a play produced in London a few years ago, the family gramophone was always referred to as *Robert*, and I know a house in which the telephone is *Peter*. When I was for some weeks an inmate of a nursing-home, one of the nurses regularly called a hot-water bottle *Tommy*, while another preferred the name *Monty*. My own children called a dodging patch of sunshine on the nursery wall an *Anthony dizzer*, nor could the most subtly diplomatic interrogation ever discover the origin of the name.

As a rule, only the most familiar names are used in this way. When an out-of-the-way name crops up, it may sometimes be possible to find a reason for its selection. The tower of the Abbey church of Middelburg, Holland, is *de lange Jan*, i.e. long John, a name probably taken at random. The water-tower which ruins a distant view of Colchester is *Jumbo*, and thereby hangs a true tale. Just fifty years ago the British public indulged in one of those fits of hysteria which help us to realize the infinite possibilities of democracy. The dread edict had gone forth that *Jumbo*,[1] most elephantine of the Zoo elephants, was to be sold to Barnum. The great heart of the people was deeply stirred, and *Jumbo*, *Jumboesque*, *Jumbomania*, etc., were added to the English vocabulary (see the Oxford Dictionary). Just then Colchester decided to build a water-tower at the top of its picturesque High Street. One indignant city-father described the monstrosity as a ' great Jumbo ', and *Jumbo* it is called to this day. Perhaps some etymologist of the future will explain it as a ' corruption ' of *Jean le Beau* ! Has not *Shakespeare* been derived from *Jacques Pierre*, *Charing* from *chère reine*, and even *Coldharbour* [2] from *col d'arbres* ?

---

[1] The name of the animal was perhaps suggested by *Mumbo-Jumbo*, the mysterious Nigerian divinity invented by husbands for the control of recalcitrant wives. He is mentioned by English travellers of the early 18th century.

[2] The origin of the name is quite well known. It is practically synonymous with *Caldecote* and means a place of shelter which does not provide food and fire. See the Oxford Dictionary, a work apparently not accessible to the eminent K.C. who writes to the ' papers ' to suggest derivation from Anglo-Saxon *col*, coal, *har*, ancient, *bearh*, mound !

The old etymologists never knew when they were beaten. They excelled in the ' anecdotic ' and trusted to their own inventive powers. The origin of *humbug*, an 18th-century word, is unknown, but one William Pulleyn, who published an Etymological Compendium about the middle of the 19th century, is quite clear as to the derivation of what De Quincey calls ' this virtuous and inexorable word '—

> The derivation of this word, now in such common use, is not generally known ; but it is of Scottish origin. There was in former years residing in the neighbourhood of the Mearns, in Scotland, a gentleman of landed property, whose name was Hume or Home ; and his estate was known as the Bogue. From the great falsehoods that ' Hume of the Bogue ' was in the habit of relating about himself, his family, and everything connected with him, it soon became customary, when persons heard anything that was remarkably extravagant and absurd, to say, ' That is a Hume o' the Bogue '. The expression spread like wildfire over the whole country ; and those who did not understand the origin of this phrase and applied it only to any extravagant action or saying, contracted it into one word, and corrupted it to Humbug.

Another theorist identifies *humbug* with *Hamburg*, ' from which town so many false bulletins and reports came during the War in the last century ', and a third with *Wilhelm Homburg*, a German chemist of the 17th century. All three fantasies illustrate the popular tendency to connect mysterious words with individual names, documentary evidence being supplied in the shape of some absurd invention and all phonetic rules being set at defiance.

In a book [1] on words derived from names pub-

---

[1] Charnock, Verba Nominalia.

M

lished in 1856, we read that *mayonnaise* [1] is ' properly *bayonnaise*, so called from *Bayonne*, where it was first made '. Initial *b-* does not readily become initial *m-*, though one could imagine a nation with endemic cold in the head bringing about the opposite transformation. The same authority tells us that the *Martello towers*, of which a few still linger on the south coast, are ' so named from Martello, a Corsican engineer, the first inventor '. This ' Corsican engineer ', more invented than inventing, has recently cropped up in the ' correspondence column '. *Martello* is a corruption of *Mortella*, from *Cape Mortella* (i.e. myrtle) in Corsica, where stood a tower which gave the British fleet and troops much trouble in 1793–4. *Neddy*, an old word for a life-preserver (cf. *jemmy*), is explained in Hotten's Slang Dictionary (1864) as ' a contraction of *Kennedy*, the name of the first man, it is said in St. Giles's, who had his head broken by a poker '.

The correspondence columns of our middlebrow weeklies and of our two Sunday papers are the happy hunting-ground of the amateur etymologist. A few years ago he published the discovery that *nap*, a short sleep, was derived from *Napoleon's* power of sleeping at will. It being pointed out by a sane contributor that *nap* can be traced back to

[1] Generally believed to commemorate the French capture of *Mahon*, Minorca, in 1756. Victories have often been commemorated in this way, e.g. *magenta*, from the defeat of the Austrians by the French (1859) at *Magenta* (North Italy), and French *mazagran*, coffee in a glass, from an exploit at *Mazagran* (Algeria). But the *Waterloo Cup* owes its name to the accident of its having been instituted at the *Waterloo* Hotel, Liverpool.

Anglo-Saxon, our friend retorted that the Anglo-Saxon word only applied to an involuntary sleep— ' We have therefore an instance, rare if not unique in etymology, of two words spelt and pronounced in the same way, derived from two completely different sources, but with meanings so similar that they may be confused even by an expert ' (!) Another philologist tells us that the word *wallop*, to beat soundly, is derived from *Sir John Wallop*, ' a valiant commander in Henry VIII.'s time', who distinguished himself by ' walloping ' the French. That being so, it is curious that the word is not found so used before the 19th century. Not that a gap of a few centuries ever worries our friend. For about the last twenty years the name *Nosey Parker* has been applied to the unduly inquisitive. The Oxford Dictionary is not acquainted with the gentleman, nor does it record *nos(e)y*, except in the senses of having a large nose or being sensitive to bad smells. There is, however, a slang *nose* meaning an informer, a *copper's nark* [1], so one might conjecture that this *Mr. Parker* belongs to thieves' slang.[2] According, however, to our amateur philologist—

There is no mystery about the origin of the term Nosey Parker. It was born in the spacious days of Queen Elizabeth, when the original Parker was her first archbishop of Canterbury. . . . Matthew Parker was a human ferret. He lived his life prying into other people's affairs. But it was during his metro-political visitation of the province of Canterbury . . . that the long archiepiscopal nose of Matthew Parker gave him the name that still describes the persistently inquisitive.

[1] Romany *nāk*, nose.
[2] Unless *Parker* is an imitative spelling of *pauker*, from dialect *pauk*, to be inquisitive.

The mention of *Nosey Parker* suggests a digression on the curious additions which the army and navy regularly give to the commoner type of surname. The following list is probably far from complete— *Aggie Weston, Betsy Gay, Blanco White, Bodger Lees, Bogey Harris, Brigham Young, Buck Taylor, Busky Smith, Chats Harris, Charley Peace, Daisy Dean, Darky Smith, Dinghy Reed, Dodger Green, Dolly Grey, Doughy Baker, Dusty Jordan (Miller, Rhodes, Smith), Edna May, Fanny Adams (Fields), Flapper Hughes, Ginger Jones, Granny Henderson, Gunboat Smith, Hooky Walker, Jigger Lees, Jimmy Green, Johnny Walker, Jumper Collins (Cross), Kitty Wills, Knocker White (Walker), Lackery Wood, Lottie Collins, Mouchy Reeves, Nobby Clark (Ewart, Hewart, Hewett), Nocky Knight, Nutty Cox, Piggy May, Pincher Martin, Pony Moore, Rattler Morgan, Sheeny Bryant, Shiner Bright (Black, Bryant, Green, White, Wright), Shover Smith, Shorty Wright, Slinger Wood, Smoky Holmes, Smudger Smith, Snip Parsons (Taylor), Spiky Sullivan, Spokey Wheeler, Spud Murphy, Taffy Jones (Owen, etc.), Timber Wood, Tom King, Topper Brown, Tottie Bell, Tug Wilson, Wheeler Johnson, Wiggy Bennett.* Some of these are self-explanatory, nor is the transition from *Parsons* to *Snip* outside etymological experience. Others (*Nobby Ewart, Pincher Martin*) are traditionally connected with well-known officers. *Agnes Weston* was ' the sailors' friend ', and *Fanny Adams*, also a naval name for tinned meat, was the victim of an early trunk murder. *Lackery* is Hindustani *lakri*, wood. When they are all elucidated, we shall perhaps be nearer to the origin of *Nosey Parker* !

There are a few words which are discussed periodically, e.g. about Derby Day some one usually raises the question of the origin of the *welsher*, formerly *welcher*. The Oxford Dictionary cannot help us, but a Welsh contributor to a Sunday paper can—

Welsher, as applied on the race-course, has no reference to the Welsh, but was coined after an incident which happened many years ago on Epsom Downs, the subject of the term being one Bob Welch. Mr. Welch had ' laid the odds ', found he could not pay up, and so, cleared off. His emulators have ever since been dubbed Welchers. Unfortunately, the term is invariably misspelt.

One would like to know more of *Mr. Bob Welch* and to have those ' many years ago ' more exactly dated. But chronology is not a strong point with the volunteer instructor of the public. He prefers to imitate the vagueness of Grose, who tells us that the saying ' before one could say Jack Robinson ' immortalizes ' a very volatile gentleman of that appellation, who would call on his neighbours, and be gone before his name could be announced '.

To the student there is something almost awe-inspiring in the martial impatience with which the amateur cuts the Gordian knots of etymology. He is equally strong in history and biography. Before me lies a cutting containing replies to a question as to the identity of the painter who, asked how he mixed his colours, replied, ' With brains '. Five authorities attribute the saying to five painters—Opie, Etty, Fuseli, Turner and Reynolds. The most modest of the five has ' always understood '.

The others ain't arguing, they're a-telling you.
Perhaps one of them is right.

A stock problem is *Tommy Atkins*. It is not a
problem to etymologists, because the origin of the
name is quite well-known and capable of documentary proof. A War Office circular, dated
August 31, 1815, ordered that every soldier should
keep a kind of account-book. As the soldier of
that day was often illiterate, there was attached
to the circular a specimen page with the heading
' Description, Service, etc. of Thomas Atkins,
Private No. 6 Troop, 6th Reg^t. of Dragoons.'
From that date *Thomas Atkins*, as a specimen name,
was regularly used in circulars of a similar type.
It might just as well have been *Alfred Baker*, but it
wasn't. The Oxford Dictionary's first record of
Tommy Atkins, British soldier, is from G. A. Sala
(1883), but the general popularity of the name dates
from the early works of Mr. Rudyard Kipling. A
very full account of the whole matter will be found
in the Oxford Dictionary, which one imagines had
not been consulted by the gentleman who writes—

Thomas Atkins was the name of a sentry who, when the
Europeans in Lucknow were flying, refused to leave his post and
so perished. After that it became the fashion to speak of a
conspicuously heroic soldier in the fight with the rebels as a
' regular Tommy Atkins '.

No doubt the same authority could tell us why
the ' lower deck ' calls the Royal Navy *Andrew*,
and trace the genealogy of the apparently Irish
warrior to whom we owe ' doing *Paddy Doyle* ' as
a euphemism for doing ' time ' in the cells.

Here is a geographical fantasy on the name of *Liverpool*. It may be said, *en passant*, that the origin of this name has busied some of the best brains in the world of learning and that it still remains an unsolved problem, though apparently crystal-clear to the writer of the following lines—

The name of Liverpool is of Irish origin and commemorates the fact of the occupation of that part of the Mersey shore on which Liverpool now stands by an Irish outcast and his following in the 5th century, Leaoir Macmannimin. . . . He was banished to what is now the Isle of Man, so called after the McManimin part of his name, and from there he raided the English coast and caused the pool of the Mersey where he landed to be called his or Lear's Pool. A bowdlerized story of his life is to be found in Shakespeare's King Lear.

When we come to the gentleman who solemnly derives *Rotten Row* from Egyptian *Rut-en-Ra*, the Gateway of Ra, the Sun-god, with the comment that '*route-en-* (not *du*) *Roi* has for some time been considered a doubtful explanation', we seem to have touched bottom.

The question naturally suggests itself—Who invents all these futilities? Is there some secret factory where half-wits are set to work by the Moriarty of a gang engaged in 'uttering' etymological fictions, or do the writers of these letters evolve their 'anecdotes' from their own inner consciousness? Do they believe in them themselves—Fingunt simul creduntque? Is it a complex, or an inhibition, or a morbid libido, or what, in the name of Grimm's law, is it? And why do editors admit such stuff into their columns? The specimens given are taken at random, and it is time to stop. It will be noticed that no names or periodicals are mentioned; not that there would be any danger of hurting our lunatic contributor's feelings, for he can be trusted not to cramp his style by consulting any book which contains reasonably up-to-date information on matters etymological.

I have only twice intervened modestly in such discussions. Once, when the South African word *scoff*, to eat, was explained in one of our Sunday papers as the acrostic, *S.C.O.F.F.*, of *Senior Commissariat Officers Field Force*, I ventured to point out, veiled in the decent obscurity of initials, that *scoff* has been good South African Dutch since the 18th century and good European Dutch [1] from time immemorial. Shortly afterwards our other Sunday paper printed the following effusion from a belted knight—

The name of the famous old black German rye-bread, Pumpernickel, had a humorous origin. Napoleon, during one of his campaigns, was given this Schwarzbrot as a treat; not caring for the stuff, he gave it to his favourite charger Nicol, with the cynical remark ' C'est bon pour Nicol '. Indiscriminate in the use of their B's and P's, rather amused at Napoleon's bad taste, the Germans nicknamed the despised bread ' Pumpernickel '.

Still veiled in the decent obscurity of initials, I hazarded the observation that *pumpernickel* was known to English travellers before Napoleon was born, that it is found in German in the 17th century, that *Nickel* is a common pet-form of *Nicholas* and that the word is a humorous coinage of the same

[1] The modern form is *schoft*, fourth part of a day. Theoretically the day was divided into four spells of work, interrupted by four meals.

type as our own *brown George* or the French *gros-Guillaume* (p. 59, n. 1).   My letter did not attain the honour of insertion, the editor presumably feeling that belted knights should not be contradicted by the untitled.   Or perhaps the old maxim—' Populus vult decipi . . .' is felt to be as appropriate to etymology as to politics.

CHAPTER XIII

SHAKESPEARE AND WAGSTAFF

IN no region of word-lore has the amateur philologist done more deadly work than in the
history of our surnames. Bardsley, in his valuable
Dictionary of English and Welsh Surnames, says of
Shakespeare, ' It is impossible to retail all the nonsense that has been written about this name. Silly
guessing has run riot on the subject. Never a name
in English nomenclature so simple or so certain in
its origin. It is simply what it looks—*shake-spear* '.
To this it may be added that no European philologist of any reputation would dissent from this
opinion. This form of nickname, verb and object
(cf. *stopgap, daredevil, makeshift, sawbones, killjoy*,
etc.), is represented by hundreds of surnames in
the chief European languages and by thousands in
medieval records, the large majority of them having
proved too crude or too complicated to survive in
the surnominal struggle for life, e.g. our medieval
Cullebulluc (kill-bullock) has disappeared, though
the French *Tubeuf* still flourishes and is appropriately represented by a butcher in the *Bottin* [1]
for 1907. Early examples are the Norman *Taillefer*,[2]

---

[1] The Paris Directory, now in its 135th year, published by
Didot Bottin.   [2] Cf. the Italian name *Tagliaferro*.

now *Telfer*, and *Taillebois*, now *Tallboys*. English
are *Doolittle*, *Turnpenny*, *Lovejoy*, *Breakspear*,
Drinkwater, *Gathergood*, the hoarder, and *Scatter-
good*, the prodigal.   These and hundreds of others
are plentifully attested in the medieval rolls, from
the 12th century onward.   They are never preceded
by *de* or *atte*, so cannot be local; they are never
found as first names, so cannot be ' corruptions ' of
baptismal names; they are never preceded by *le* or
the, so cannot be occupational.   Therefore, to anyone who understands what is meant by philological
evidence, they are nicknames, easily paralleled in
other languages, e.g. *Drinkwater*, perhaps the commonest English surname of this type, has as equiva-
lents French *Boileau*, Italian *Bevilacqua*, German
Trinkwasser, Dutch *Drinkwater*.[1]

The etymology of *Shakespeare* has long been for
philologists a *chose jugée*, but now comes along a
theorist, whom, in accordance with the best modern
legal precedent, we will call Mr. X, to tell us that
we are all wrong, and that the existence of the
corresponding German *Schüttespeer* and the Italian
Crollalanza means nothing.   Briefly put, Mr. X's
view seems to be that the English name *Saxby* may

[1] It is probable that such names had a double meaning,
literal and ironic, so that the first *Shake-spear* may have been
either a swashbuckler or a timid individual.   It will be remembered that little David Copperfield, *en route* for his boarding-
school, was addressed by the waiter as ' six-foot '.   From the
name of the stoical Roman philosopher *Seneca* is derived Portuguese *sengo*, sententious, which has also in dialect the sense of
humbug and idiot.   Italian *seneca*, pale man, is an allusion to
his suicide, by opening his veins, which led early philologists
to explain the name as *se necans*, self-slaying !

have been corrupted in French to *Saquespee*, and
then in English to *Shakespeare*. The latter may
also be of local origin, or be derived from an Anglo-
Saxon personal name compounded from *seax*, knife,
' or the even more common prototheme *Sige* '.
Finally ' it seems not unlikely that the name *Shakespeare* is derived from several distinct sources '.
Similar theories are propounded for the equally
obvious *Shakeshaft* and *Shacklock*.

All this is, of course, etymological moonshine. It
may be conceded that *Shakespeare* could have
occasionally interchanged with *Saquespee*, the names
having enough superficial likeness of sound and
sense to be confused at a period when the surname
was a very loose adjunct of the font-name. We find,
for instance, the compromise *Sakespere*, and even
Drawspere and *Drawespe*. Both *Saquespee* and the
synonymous *Draweswerd* [1] were well established
medieval names, the former being found as early as
the 12th century, e.g. Jordan Sacheespee is in the
Pipe Rolls. It survives in French *Sacquepé* (Bottin,
1907), but in England has been absorbed by *Saxby*.
Mr. X tells us that ' *Sakeespee* is approximately
French '. Rather more than ' approximately ', since
sachier (Norman *saquier*, *sakier*) *l'espee* is as common in Old French romance as to *draw the sword*
is in medieval English.

The existing *Shake-* names are *Shacklock*, *Shake-*

---

[1] During the bi-lingual period, i.e. c. 1066–1300, French surnames run parallel with native surnames in England. It is
quite possible that the same man was known both as *Saquespee*
and *Draweswerd*.

lance (very rare), *Shakeshaft* or *Shackshaft*, *Shake-speare*. Apparently obsolete are *Shakesheath*, *Shake-staff*. There are one or two more which I omit *pudoris causa*. Now, if we look up the transitive verb *shake* in the Oxford Dictionary, we find as earliest senses to brandish, to agitate (some part of the body), to wag, flap, etc. And the oldest quotations are—

> Heo scæken on heore honden speren swithe stronge.
> > (Layamon, 26481.)
> > Schaftes thai gun schake.
> > > (Sir Tristram, 885.)
> > Thei schulen schake lockis, as the whelpis of liouns.[1]
> > > (Wyclif; Jeremiah li. 38.)

From which it may be reasonably inferred that the ' shaking ' of *spears*, *shafts* and *locks* was not a practice unknown to the Middle Ages ! With *Break-spear*, a name of similar type, one may compare the once common *Briselance*, still found in France. It is quite obvious to normal intelligence that *Shake-spear* belongs to the same type as *Taille-fer*, the still more formidable *Mange-fer*, the existing German name *Hauenschild* (swash-buckler), and its Middle English parallel *Crakesheld* (crack-shield). We may regret that our ancestors were so fond of shaking, breaking, and cracking, but we cannot help it.

The early *Shakespears* earned their name in the same way as the early *Benbows*, who, in the Middle Ages, bore the nickname *bende-bowe*. Nor had Robert Greene any illusions as to the *shake* of *Shake-speare*, when he spitefully described him (in a Groat's worth of Wit, c. 1590) as ' in his owne conceit the

[1] Vulgate, ' Excutient comas quasi catuli leonum.'

only shake-scene in a countrie'. Finally, Mr. X
himself supplies us with most valuable evidence in
the surname of one *Fewterspere*, whom he has discovered in the Cheshire Plea Rolls for 1362. If we
look up *fewter* in the Oxford Dictionary, we find the
definition ' to put (a spear) into the " fewter ", or
rest ', with four quotations, in all of which the word
is naturally associated with *spear*, the last in date
being from Spenser—

> Which being yeelded, he his threatfull speare
> Gan fewter, and against her fiercely ran.
> (Faerie Queene, IV. vi. 10.)

If a medieval Englishman could be named from
' fewtering ' his spear, one imagines he might also
be named from the more ostentatious gesture of
' shaking ' it.

With the *Shake-* names go the *Wag-* names, of
which the commonest is *Wagstaff*, which looks like
a kind of Sancho Panza counterpart of the quixotic
Shakespeare. But *wag* had no ludicrous suggestion
in Middle English. Its oldest transitive sense was
identical with that of *shake*, i.e. to brandish (a
weapon) defiantly. It is used with *weapon* in
Havelok (c. 1300), the Oxford Dictionary's next
quotation being from Coverdale (1535)—

> Be not afrayde for the Kinge of the Assirians—he shal wagg
> [A.V. lift up] his staff at thee, but, etc.
> (Isaiah x. 24.)

Mr. X tells us that *Wagstaff* ' might well be a personal
name and it also has the appearance of being local ',
but I imagine that it would be hard to put forward
similar conjectures for the synonymous Reginald

Waggebastun,[1] who is registered in the Close Rolls for 1227–31. Less common are *Waghorn*, also recorded early, and *Wagspear*, which seems to be obsolete. I am not sure whether *Wagtail* still exists, though an undergraduate of some forty years ago, who rejoiced in the picturesque surname *Shuffle-bottom*, was occasionally addressed by this euphemistic equivalent. The Oxford Dictionary's records of *wagtail* are for 1510 (the bird), 1592 (an improper lady), 1605 (a contemptuous name applied by Kent to Goneril's steward, in King Lear, ii. 2) ; but *Wagtail* was already a surname [2] in the 12th century.

To conclude, the name *Shakespeare* is derived from the habit or gesture of shaking a spear and the name *Wagstaff* from wagging a staff. Anyone who wishes to establish their local origin must furnish us with medieval examples of William atte Schake-spere or John de Waggestæf. If they are to be regarded as personal names, we must ask for documentary records of Schakesperius fil. Gullielmi or of Waggestæffius carpentarius. Most convincing of all would be such an entry as Schakesperius fil. Waggestæffii !

The foregoing paragraphs may seem rather a departure from the smiling serenity with which one

[1] With this compare the Middle English *trailbaston*, the name of a class of violent wrong-doers, temp. Edward I, who were the subject of special legislation. The English rendering *Draghbatte* is found as a medieval nickname.

[2] i.e. it is registered as a man's name in the Pipe Rolls. It should be understood that the medieval Englishman, especially of the plebs, might be known by more than one surname, according as it pleased his neighbours or the officials to describe him in terms of his parentage, residence, occupation or characteristics.

should regard the antics of the amateur etymologist.
It is obvious that the bottom of the world need not
drop out because a few guileless souls are induced
to believe nonsense about surnames; but, all the
same, one feels that those in quest of linguistic
knowledge have a right to expect that printed
information should approximate to the present
state of philological science. It is also to be re-
gretted that, in England alone of European countries, etymological corpses which were decently
buried half a century ago can be disinterred and
their resurrection amiably acclaimed by a chorus
of ' irresponsible, indolent reviewers '.

INDEX

Made and Printed in Great Britain by Butler & Tanner Ltd., Frome and London